THE EUROPEAN
UNION

The opinions in this book are our own, and should not be
interpreted as being those of the European Commission

AR

SAB

337.142
R772e

PROFESSIONAL
PAPERBACKS

THE EUROPEAN UNION

A GUIDE THROUGH THE EC/EU MAZE

SIXTH EDITION

Alex Roney and Stanley Budd

INSTITUTE OF DIRECTORS

**KOGAN
PAGE**

79669

LONDON, UK • NEW HAMPSHIRE, USA • NEW DELHI, INDIA

YOURS TO HAVE AND TO HOLD
BUT NOT TO COPY

First published in 1985 by Inro Press, Edinburgh
Second edition published in 1987 by Kogan Page Ltd
Third edition 1989
Fourth edition 1991
Fifth edition 1994
Sixth edition 1998

Kogan Page Limited
120 Pentonville Road
London N1 9JN
© Alex Roney, 1998

Kogan Page Limited
163 Central Avenue, Suite 4
Dover, NH 03820, USA

British Library Cataloguing in Publication Data

A CIP record for this book is available from the British Library.

ISBN 0 7494 2117 7

Typeset by Saxon Graphics Ltd, Derby.
Printed and bound in Great Britain by Biddles Ltd, Guildford and King's Lynn.

Contents

How to Use the Book

This book is in nine sections – the last being sources of information, useful addresses, e-mail numbers, websites and helplines – together with lists of free EC publications available and some useful books.

The text given in the body of the book is intended as an overview to give a broad understanding and to guide readers towards sources of further information.

Foreword

So much has happened since the original edition of this book that it was time, in order to do justice to the memory of Stanley Budd, to revise it substantially.

The EU, now with 15 Member States, has moved on significantly. The Single Market is here and accepted by many, with increased movement in people, capital, goods, and services. Some barriers to trade remain, but they are falling. The internal borders in the EU have dropped visibly, and the EU citizen has been born. The EU is deepening, and European Monetary Union (EMU) and the single currency will start on 1 January 1999 with 11 Member States participating.

The European Union is also widening, and accession negotiations have started with 6 of the 11 applicant states, so it is a time of change. The powers of the European Parliament have increased, and further institutional change is necessary to enable effective decision-making when the next enlargement takes place. The available funds are having to be carefully managed to enable the EU to take the strain of absorbing and supporting the new members.

The enormous problem of unemployment in the EU has meant that the drive to encourage proper economic development and the right business climate to create new jobs can be seen in the different action plans and programmes. Account has had to be taken of the competitiveness of the EU in global trade, and global trade agreements have been negotiated through the World Trade Organization which will impact significantly on manufacturers, on business people and thus on all their employees in the EU.

The need to protect the environment is no longer seen as a 'cranky' issue; it is now accepted, and the threat of global warming and pollution is being addressed.

The vast amount of information about Europe (and everything else) which increases daily has brought about possibly the biggest change of all to the lives and working patterns of the citizens of the EU – the rushing advent of the Information Society. This has meant that the only reasonable way in which information can be managed is by making it available via electronic databases – most conveniently via the Internet. Thus the emphasis of the last part of this book has changed. Guidance concerning some available publications and where to get them will be mentioned, but so too will be various website enquiry points, and specialist databases where information may be accessed.

However, the first step is to know enough to enable you to ask the right questions. I hope that this latest edition of this well-known book will help you to do so.

Alex Roney
September 1998

Acronyms and Abbreviations

ACP	African, Caribbean and Pacific members of the Lomé Convention
ADAPT	Programme to forecast labour to adjust to industrial changes
ALTENER	Alternative energy programme
ASEAN	Association of South East African Countries
BCC	Business Cooperation Centre
BEUC	European Bureau of Consumers' Unions
BICEPS	Bioinformatics Collaborative European Programme and Strategy
BOTB	British Overseas Trade Board
BRITE	Basic Research in Industrial Technologies for Europe
CADDIA	Cooperation in Automation for Data and Documentation for Import
CAP	Common Agricultural Policy
CCT/CET	Common Customs Tariff (between the EC aand third countries)
CDPC	Committee on Problems of Crime
CE	Mark certifying compliance with the EC Provisions
CEDEFOP	European Centre for the Development of Vocational Training
CEEC	Central and Eastern European Countries
CEN	European Committee for Standardisation
CENELEC	European Committee for Electrotechnical Standardisation
CERD	European Committee for Research and Development
CFP	Common Fisheries Policy
CFSP	Common Foreign and Security Policy
CIS	Commonwealth of Independent States (part of former USSR)
CIT	Consultative Committee on Innovation and Technology
CODEST	Committee for the European Development of Science and Technology
COI	Commission on Information
COM or COMDOC	Commission Documents
COMETT	Community in Education and Training for Technology

COPA	Committee of Agricultural Organisations in the European Community
CORDI	Advisory Committee on Industrial Research and Development
COREPER	The Committee of Permanent Representatives
COST	Committee for European Cooperation in the Field of Scientific Research
CREST	Committee on Scientific and Technical Research
CRONOS	Community Statistical Office Computerised Economic Data Bank
CSCE	Conference on Security and Cooperation in Europe
CUBE	Concertation Unit for Biotechnology
DG	Directorate-General
DRIVE	Dedicated Road Safety Systems and Intelligent Vehicles in Europe
DTI	Department of Trade and Industry
EAEC	European Atomic Energy Community (EURATOM)
EAGGF	(FEOGA –see below)
EBN	European Business and Innovation Centre Network
EBRD	European Bank for Reconstruction and Development
EC	European Community
ECAS	European Citizens Action Service
ECB	European Central Bank
ECDIN	Environmental Chemical Data and Information Network
ECJ	European Court of Justice
ECOSOC	See ESC
ECSC	European Coal and Steel Community
ECTRA	European Committee for Telecommunication Regulatory Affairs
ECU	European Currency Unit
ED	European Documentation (a series – see page 000)
EDC	European Documentation Centre
EDC	European Development Community
EDF	European Development Fund
EEA	European Economic Area
EEA	European Environment Agency
EEIG	European Economic Interest Grouping
EF	European File (a series – see page 000)
EFTA	European Free Trade Association
EIB	European Investment Bank
EMS	European Monetary System
EMU	Economic and Monetary Union
EP	European Parliament
ERASMUS	European Community Action Scheme for Mobility of University Students
ERDF	European Regional Development Fund

ERM	Exchange Rate Mechanism
ESC	Economic and Social Committee
ESCAP	European Social and Community Action Programme
ESCB	European System of Central Banks
ESF	European Social Fund
ESPRIT	European Strategic Programme for Research and Development in Information Technology
ETUC	European Trades Union Confederation
EU	European Union
EURAM	European Research in Advanced Materials
EURATOM	European Atomic Energy Community (EAEC)
EUREKA	European Research Coordination Agency
EURES	European Employment Services
EURES	European Employment Services Network
Euro	The name of the single currency
EURODAC	European system to deal with multiple asylum requests
EUROFER	European Confederation of the Iron and Steel Industry
EURONET-DIANE	Direct Information Access Network for Europe
EUR-OP	Office for Official Publications of the European Communities
EUROPMI	European Committee for Small and Medium-sized Industry
EUROPOL	European Police Office
EUROSTAT	European Community Statistics
EUROTRA	Community Programme for a Machine Translation System of Advanced Design
EURYDICE	Education Information Network in the European Community
EVCA	European Venture Capital Association
EXPROM	Executive Training Programme
FAST	Forecasting and Assessment in the Field of Science and Technology
FEOGA	French acronym for EAGGF – European Agricultural Guidance and Guarantee Fund
GATT	General Agreement in Tariff and Trade
GSP	Generalised System of Preferences
IBC	Integrated Broad-band Communication
INSIS	International Information System
IRDAC	Industrial Research and Development Advisory Committee
ISDN	Integrated Services Digital Network (narrow-band telecommunication)
IT	Information Technologies
ITTTF	Information Technology and Telecommunications Task Force
JET	Joint European Torus
JRC	Joint Research Centre (at Ispra, Italy)
MCAs	Monetary Compensatory Amounts

MFA	Multi-Fibre Arrangement
NAFO	North Atlantic Fisheries Organisation
NASCO	North Atlantic Salmon Conservation Organisation
NATO	North Atlantic Treaty Organization
NCI (or NIC)	New Community Instrument (also known as the Ortoli Facility)
OJ	Official Journal
RACE	Research into Advanced Communications in Europe
R and D	Research and Development
RDF	See ERDF
RECHAR	Programme for the Conversion of Mining Areas
RECIFER	Programme to Assist Steel Producing Regions
RECITE	Regions and Cities of Europe
RENAVAL	Programme to Assist Shipbuilding Industry
SEA	Single European Act
SITPRO	Simplification of Trade Procedure
SLIM	Initiative for Simpler Legislation for the Internal Market
SMEs	Small and Medium-sized Enterprises
SOCRATES	A wide-ranging programme in the higher educational sector
SPRINT	Strategic Programme for Innovation and Technology Transfer in Europe
STABEX	Stabilisation of Export Earnings (in the ACP countries)
STAR	Programme for access to advanced telecommunications in certain regions of the Community
STCELA	Standing Technological Conference of European Local Authorities
TACs	Total Allowable Catches in Fisheries Policy
TED	Tenders Electronic Daily
TELL	Treaty on European Union
TENs	Trans European Networks – This relates to infrastructure, IT and energy links
THERMIE	Programme promoting energy technology in the EU
UCITS	Undertakings for Collective Investment in Transferable Securities
UKREP	UK Permanent Representative (or Representation)
UNICE	Conference of Industries of the European Community
VALOREN	Development of certain regions of the Community by exploiting indigenous energy potential
WEA	Western European Union
WTO	World Trade Organization

Dates to be remembered in the progress towards European union

1951

Belgium, France, Germany, Italy, Netherlands and Luxembourg (the Six) sign the Treaty to establish the European Coal and Steel Community (ECSC) in Paris.

1954

The Brussels Treaty Organisation of 1948 (Belgium, France, Netherlands and the UK) was extended to include Germany and Italy to become the Western European Union (WEU).

1957

The Rome Treaty to establish the European Economic Community (EEC), and the EURATOM Treaty to establish the European Atomic Energy Community were signed in Rome by the Six. These entered into force on 1 January 1958. The EEC and EURATOM Commissions came into being.

1962

The Common Agricultural Policy (CAP) was established.

1965

A Treaty to merge the executive functions of the executives of the European Coal and Steel, EEC and EURATOM Communities was signed, but came into force in 1967.

1968

Customs duties in intra-Community trade were finally abolished for manufactured goods, and common external tariff was introduced.

1970
A Treaty to provide for extended budgetary powers of the EP and introduction of an own resources system was agreed in Luxembourg.

1972
The Treaty on the Accession of Denmark, Ireland, Norway and the UK was signed.
The Exchange Rate Mechanism (ERM) often referred to as 'the Snake' was established.

1973
On 1 January 1973 Denmark, Ireland and the UK joined the Six. Norway had not proceeded to accession.

1974
The Heads of State and Government of the Nine agree to meet regularly as the European Council, and agreed to establish the European Regional Development Fund (ERDF). It was decided there should be direct elections for MEPs. These were first held in 1979.

1975
A Treaty to establish the Court of Auditors, and to give the EP wider budgetary powers was signed (in force 1 June 1997).

1978
The European Monetary System was proposed. It started operating in 1979.

1979
The Treaty for Accession of Greece was signed. Greece joined on 1 January 1981.

1986
On 1 January 1996 Portugal and Spain joined the Community, and shortly afterwards the Twelve signed the Single European Act which entered into force in July 1987.

1987
Turkey applied to join the Twelve. It was agreed that the WEU should present joint security policy.

1989
Austria applied to join the Twelve, and the Berlin Wall was brought down.

1990

It was agreed that the European Bank of Reconstruction and Development (EBRD) should be established.

East Germany was once more joined to West Germany. Cyprus and Malta applied to join the EC.

The Schengen Agreement on the elimination of border controls for internal borders was signed by Belgium, France, Germany, Luxembourg and the Netherlands following on from the Schengen Accord signed in 1985. These five were later joined by other Member States. Schengen officially came into effect in its signatory states on 26 March 1995, but has now been incorporated as an obligation into the Amsterdam Treaty with special arrangements for Denmark, Ireland and the UK.

Cyprus and Malta applied to join the Community, Malta later withdrawing its application.

1991

Sweden applied to join the EC.

1992

The Treaty on European Union was signed at Maastricht.

The Agreement on the establishment of an European Economic Area was signed, which was an agreement between all the governments concerned to extend the Single Market to EFTA countries who wished to participate to make a larger trading block. It came into effect on 1 January 1994 and now includes all EU countries plus Iceland, Liechtenstein and Norway (Switzerland retains observer status). This means that the free movement of persons, goods, services and capital extends to these countries, but some provisions do not apply to them eg they do not have to levy VAT.

Liechtenstein applied to join the Community.

1993

1 January 1993 The Single Market came into being.

1 November 1993 The TEU came into force.

1994

Hungary and Poland applied to join the EU.

Treaties of Accession to the Community were signed by Austria, Finland, Norway and Sweden.

1995

1 January 1995 Austria, Finland and Sweden joined the EU (but not

Norway). Bulgaria, Estonia, Latvia, Lithuania and Slovakia applied to join the EU.

1996
Czech Republic and Slovenia applied to join.

1997
A Treaty for Europe: the Treaty on European Union referred to as the Amsterdam Treaty, was signed in June 1997. This will come into effect when ratified by all Member States. At the time of writing, full ratification is close. Agenda 2000, the strategy for strengthening growth, competitiveness and employment, and for widening and strengthening the EU into the new Millennium was presented by the Commission.

1998
Accession negotiations were launched with Cyprus, Czech Republic, Estonia, Hungary, Poland and Slovenia. The accession process has been opened with Bulgaria, Latvia, Lithuania, Romania and Slovakia.

1 January 1999
European Monetary Union is scheduled to start in all EU Members except Greece and Sweden, which did not achieve the convergence criteria. Denmark and the UK have an opt out and may join later.

Part I

The European Community and its purposes

THE BASIC FACTS

The phrases 'European Union' or 'EU', 'European Community' or 'EC' or simply 'Communities' or 'Community' are used in this book. 'European Communities' should perhaps be more exact, since there were three, the UK having been a member of all of them since 1 January 1973:

1. The European Coal and Steel Community (ECSC)
2. The European Atomic Energy Community (EURATOM)
3. The European Economic Community (EEC).

Confusingly, over the years various terms have been used, as these three Communities were developed, and now, since the Treaty on European Union, the EU is the most common, although technically that treaty does not cover all the matters previously included in the European Communities' competences, so European Community or EC is also used.

The Preamble to the European Coal and Steel Community (ECSC) Treaty succinctly outlined the intentions:

> to substitute for age-old rivalries the merging of essential interests; to create by establishing an economic Community, the basis for a broader and deeper community among the peoples long divided by bloody conflicts; and to lay the foundations for institutions which will give direction to a destiny henceforward shared.

All three Communities now share the same institutions. The principal Community institutions are:

- the Council of the European Union (previously called the Council of Ministers)
- The European Parliament to which the Commission is answerable, and which is increasingly involved in decision-making

- the Commission – effectively the EC's civil service, with very limited legislative powers
- the European Court of Justice, with jurisdiction in respect of Community treaties and legislation
- the Court of Auditors – responsible for auditing Community finances.

These are discussed in more detail in Part II.

The EC, and indeed the EU itself, owe their existence to the original initiative of a number of European statesmen (Robert Schuman, Jean Monnet, Paul-Henri Spaak and Sir Winston Churchill being the best known) who had the courage and vision to determine that a new approach was required to prevent further hostilities from breaking out in Europe.

The ECSC came first in 1951. Its aim was to lock together the coal and steel resources of Western Europe in such a way that those nation-states that possessed them could not wage war against each other. The ECSC treaty was signed in Paris (so was often called the Paris Treaty or Treaty of Paris) in 1951 by six countries: France, Germany, Italy, Belgium, The Netherlands and Luxembourg.

During the 1950s several attempts were made to integrate the armies of Western Europe which led to the formation of the Western European Union (WEU) and the North Atlantic Treaty Organization (NATO).

The success of the ECSC led the original six countries to sign the Treaty of Rome in 1957, establishing the European Economic Community, often referred to as the Common Market; and the European Atomic Energy Community, known as EURATOM. This was designed to oversee and support the development of nuclear and atomic energy for peaceful uses.

The institutions that were created to ensure the effective operation of the ECSC were merged with the institutions of EURATOM and the EEC in 1967 into a single institutional framework. However, the ECSC Treaty lapses in 2002, and its aims and mechanisms will then form part of the Community competences.

The United Kingdom (UK) declined to join the Community when it was first established, and so played no part in its development during a time when its influence could have been both positive and mutually rewarding. Initially the UK preferred membership of the European Free Trade Association (EFTA), a looser trading group, to that of the EC. EFTA then included Austria, Denmark, Finland and Sweden (who have all subsequently left it to join the EC), Iceland, Liechtenstein, Norway and Switzerland.

However, during the 1960s the UK made two attempts to join the EC, but on both occasions was refused entry into the Community, largely on the insistence of France who felt that UK membership would hamper European integration efforts. Only in 1969 after the retirement of President de Gaulle were negotiations for the enlargement of the EC to include the UK, Denmark, Ireland and Norway begun in earnest. Agreement was reached on entry terms in 1971 (Norway later deciding not to enter).

Thus the EC of six became the EC of nine with the accession of Denmark, Ireland and the UK on 1 January 1973. Throughout the 1970s the Community was confronted with a range of serious issues, in particular economic recession brought about by oil price rises in 1974, the UK referendum on continued membership of the Community in 1975, disputes over agricultural policy and budgetary contributions, and the future direction of the Community. Despite these difficulties the EC held, and still holds, attractions for many non-member countries. Greece, Portugal and Spain applied for full membership in the mid-1970s.

On 1 January 1981 Greece became the tenth member of the EC, while in January 1986 the Community was further enlarged to include Spain and Portugal. In 1990 the re-unification of Germany effectively added another country. In 1995 Austria, Finland and Sweden also joined, bringing the number of Member States to 15.

The next enlargements will encompass countries in Central and Eastern Europe and the Mediterranean. Association Agreements have been approved with 10 applicant states to assist them towards membership (Bulgaria, Czech Republic, Estonia, Hungary, Lithuania, Poland, Romania, Slovenia and Slovakia). Turkey applied to join before them – in 1987, but although they have had a customs union agreement with the EC since 1996, its accession remains a goal, partly because of concerns about breaches of human rights there, although the European Council decided in December 1997 that closer cooperation with Turkey in all areas should be pursued in order to prepare it for accession. Accession negotiations with Cyprus, who applied to join in 1990, the Czech Republic, Estonia, Hungary, Poland and Slovenia have started. Malta who also applied in 1990 has withdrawn its application for membership, but may re-apply.

THE COMMUNITY'S ROLE TODAY

The European Communities were established to put an end to the futile squandering of lives in wars which began in Europe. The means of achieving this included:

- the levelling out of inequalities between peoples and regions
- securing employment, and building prosperity within a Common Market
- Making the EC a fair trading partner and a more effective source of aid for the poorer countries of the world
- pooling the energies of Europe's peoples in common technological and industrial progress, a common agricultural policy, closer political and economic links, a better environment and a richer life.

Progress towards some of these objectives has been dramatic, but towards others rather slow.

The prosperity of the original six members of the Community increased greatly after it was formed. During the ten years before the UK joined, their exports and their gross national product rose twice as fast as the UK's, their family consumption two and a half times as fast, and their investment five times as fast. The EC is now the world's largest developed trading entity. It is the biggest single market for the developing nations. It contributes the largest share of world development aid and aid to refugees, victims of national disasters and of armed conflict.

The greatest achievement of the Community is less quantifiable. The nations of the world face, in the last decade of the twentieth century, problems at least as great as those of the previous 90-odd years. They face them, what is more, at a time when breakdown of relations between continents, or even single nations, could have bloody consequences inconceivable to our grandparents.

The two World Wars which broke out in Europe within a generation were caused, not only by real economic pressures, but also by selfishness and stupidity; not only by political dishonesty, but also by the failure of traditional diplomacy; not only because of a lack of information and communication, but also because words were used fraudulently. Treaties and agreements were broken, not only by deliberate acts of bad faith, but also because they were laden with complex protocols and understood imperfectly even by those who were involved in implementing them. Such international enforcement agencies as then existed did not work effectively.

The EU is different from the supranational groupings of the past. The discussions in Brussels may sometimes seem angry and repetitive, but by previous standards they are exceptionally well informed. National Ministers and the governments that they represent make all the important decisions, often in conjunction now with more directly elected representatives of their countries, namely the MEPs, through the European Parliament.

However, they all have the support of institutions of a new kind – planning, collecting information and opinions, drawing up blueprints, re-examining, reconciling – and doing all this from an independent standpoint.

The institutions – the Council, the European Parliament, the Commission, the European Court of Justice, and the Court of Auditors – are responsible not to governments but to the people of Europe as whole, and to the Community's democratic ideals.

If sometimes the Council's agreements are reached in ill temper and in the small hours of the morning, they are eventually enshrined in many languages and in texts agreed, word for word, by all 15 Member States.

If we read of furious demonstrations in Brussels by farmers, and consumers with opposing views, of the difficulties of reconciling the views of fishing, textile, shipbuilding or motor-vehicle industries of individual states of the EU, it is worth reminding ourselves that there we are seeing, out in the open, the sort of economic and trading problems that would be there anyway, and might be very much worse if the EU did not exist. Solving such problems may seem a noisier and more lengthy business than it was 50 years ago. That is largely because the arguments are held in public. When agreements are reached, they are public too: more honourable, more enforceable, less capable of misinterpretation, and infinitely more open and democratic.

Memories fade, but the facts are on record. Within a short time and after a bloody war, the French and Germans, the Italians and the peoples of the Benelux countries learned not only how to bury their differences and rebuild their shattered economies; they learned to trust each other more than they had done for a millennium. Those who worked for the EC during those years have every reason to be proud.

Today those working for the EU face considerable frustration. The Community remains, as it always has been, a non-stop negotiating machine, with detailed programmes and policies. It is charged with working to bring the peoples of Member States together in a range of fields. Besides the domestic problems of unemployment, employment creation and conditions, quality of life, transport, the environment, energy, agriculture, fisheries, science and technology, fair competition and economic development, there are also the wider issues of relations with other countries and the Third World, global trade relations, disaster relief, security and much more...

Reaching agreements between more member countries has proved increasingly difficult, and despite efforts to streamline decision-making, as

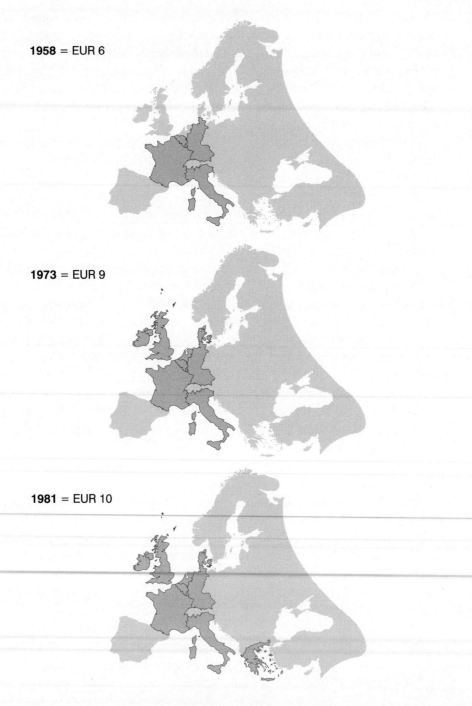

1958 = EUR 6

1973 = EUR 9

1981 = EUR 10

Figure 1 The growth of the European Community

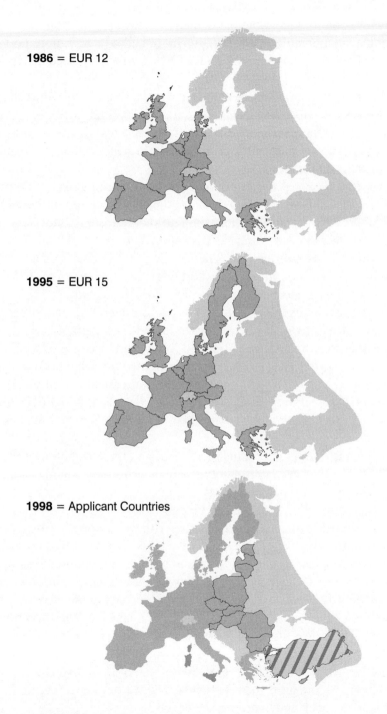

1986 = EUR 12

1995 = EUR 15

1998 = Applicant Countries

Figure 1 (contd)

Europe moves out of recession, but is then affected by recession in Japan, for example. As unemployment remains high, and so many more poorer countries wish to join, so the disciplines of EU membership become harder to tolerate.

The EU's internal policies are at the heart of its role on the world stage. Only if it lives up to its own ideals, obeys its own internal rules and is seen to do so can it offer a standard of values that the rest of the world can respect. In fact, it negotiates strongly on the world stage, with useful results for its members and citizens.

It is worth looking at the importance of the workings of the internal market, and the monitoring of its trading rules in the context of the wider aims of the EU. Free trade and fair competition are essential not only for the economic health of the internal market created in the EU, but also to restrain protectionism elsewhere. There is no point in curbing bad practices in the EU if the countries there merely export their practices to third countries and the EU sits back and lets them do it. If we demand fair treatment for our own consumers in terms of truthful labelling and advertising, control of additives, healthy preparation and packaging, and all the rest, then other nations will be obliged to follow suit, because of the EU's importance in world trade, and negotiations in the World Trade Organization forum and elsewhere. If people's rights (to education, to work, to travel freely, to equal treatment) are seen to be respected in the EU itself, then our right to expose breaches of such freedoms elsewhere becomes more valid.

All this leads to the wider aims of the EU, and the conviction of those who want to see European unity: not merely in terms of economies locked together to stop the French, Germans, Britons and other Europeans from fighting each other, but so shaped to give the fullest expression of shared ideals, mutual pride in centuries of cross-fertilized culture and history, a new explosion of creative genius based on cooperation as well as competition between peoples, and a joint approach to an exciting but increasingly unpredictable future. Such enthusiasts may be 'Eurofanatics', or they may look upon the EU as merely one avenue by which such aims may be pursued, but they believe that, at the least, there is a new approach and novel institutions which have stood up to fierce tests. There is also the pragmatic belief that the more 15 nations can agree together on a practical workday basis to establish, for example, standards of safety in industry, the more they are likely to find agreement on wider matters, on competing fairly at an international level, and in preserving peace.

The EC's plans for closer political and economic integration between its Member States continue with increased trade and travel between them, more open borders, more cooperation, and the prospect of European Monetary Union (EMU) between a hard core of Member States starting on 1 January 1999. It is time to be optimistic, and not blame the EU for all ills. It is also time to be cautious, as the motives of applicants and their ability to join this European Union have to be carefully scrutinized. Many of the answers to the difficulties and confusions of the past lie in proper education – as to the aims, duties, aspirations and capacities of this growing Community of European citizens.

PART II

The way the EC/EU works

LOCATION OF THE EC/EU'S INSTITUTIONS

- Council of the European Union (previously called Council of Ministers) – Brussels
- European Parliament – Strasbourg with some Committee meetings in Brussels, and its Secretariat in Luxembourg
- European Commission – Brussels
- European Court of Justice – Luxembourg
- (European) Court of Auditors – Luxembourg

Additional linked bodies:

- Economic and Social Committee – Brussels
- Committee of the Regions – Brussels.

PROBLEMS OF COMPARISON

It would be tempting to suggest neat parallels between the British and EC institutional structures:

- Council – Cabinet
- European Parliament – House of Commons
- European Court of Justice (ECJ) – legal system
- European Commission – Civil Service.

Unfortunately, the parallels don't work, and any attempt to explain the institutions of the Community by relating them to Westminster/Whitehall is doomed to fail.

The Council is the nearest thing the Community has to a governance, and it is by far the most powerful of the institutions. No forward action of any kind by the EC, whether it is setting prices for Community milk production, or fixing the quotas for fishing can be taken unless all 15 national governments have reached a consensus of opinion that it should happen; no major legislation can be achieved until all 15 governments have agreed to it in minute detail over the same table in the Council. But although the Council takes the Community's decisions, it does not necessarily initiate legislation. We should therefore look first at where policy-making begins. Generally speaking, the Commission proposes, and the Council disposes.

THE COUNCIL OF THE EUROPEAN UNION (COUNCIL OF MINISTERS)

The Council is the Community's principal decision-making body. It provides the framework for the participation of the governments of the Member States in the EC's decision-making process. It is the national ministers, each representing a member government who take the important Community decisions.

It is important to distinguish the Council of the EU from the European Council, which is essentially a formal summit meeting of the Heads of State and Foreign Affairs ministers, which takes place at least twice a year, usually in the country holding the Presidency at the time.

The tasks of the Council can be divided into the following:

- rights of initiative
- legislative powers
- supervisory powers over the Commission
- the right to appoint the members of the other institutions (eg the Economic and Social Committee, and the Committee of the Regions, usually on the basis of recommendations by national governments of Member States).

Decision-making and legislative processes in the EU are complex, to say the least. The procedure attached to any particular piece of legislation will depend on the relevant article of the treaty under which it is proposed. This is made more complex by the fact that sovereignty is closely guarded in some countries, such as the UK, and the decision to agree the progressive extension of straight (or simple) majority voting or even weighted or qualified majority voting to favour small countries has caused extra complications. It is perhaps useful to understand that progression towards increased use of majority voting has been the only way to avoid stagnation in decision-making at Community level, given the difficulty of achieving consensus between 15 countries, particularly given the expected enlargement of the EU in the not-too-distant future.

THE PRESIDENCY OF THE COUNCIL

A significant change in recent years has been the increasingly important role played by the Council Presidency. This development has come about as a result of the practical needs of the enlarged Community and the excessive insistence on unanimity.

Each Member State holds the Presidency of the Council for a period of six months, and it is seen an opportunity for that country to show its commitment to the EU. Six months is regarded as long enough to produce useful results, and as each country wishes to be seen to be successful, it acts as an impetus to the Community and its development. The fact that the Presidency rotates regularly, and so alternates between the larger and smaller countries also obviates any risk of hegemony. The role of the Presidency is to provide political stimuli and impartial refereeing at meetings of the Council, and to steer the Member States towards compromise. A recent example of this was the compromise accomplished by Tony Blair in achieving consensus on the appointment of the first President of the European Central Bank.

Finally, in some negotiations, the immediate past President, the present and immediate future Presidents work together. When they do this they are referred to as the Community Troica.

THE EUROPEAN COUNCIL

The European Council is the name of meetings which are effectively summits of the Heads of State or Government of the Member States. It came into being after December 1974 when President Valéry Giscard d'Estaing of France suggested that the Heads of State or Government, who had only previously met at irregular intervals, should meet regularly as the European Council, to discuss specific matters affecting the Community and questions of foreign policy. Since then, the European Council has laid down guidelines and provided a great deal of political impetus on key issues such as direct elections to the European Parliament, the accession of new countries, the creation of the European Monetary System, reform of CAP, and

Economic and Monetary Union. In June 1998 it decided that there should be a special summit to discuss institutional changes needed to improve decision-making and to bring the EU closer to the people. It also agreed that the next financial framework for the EU should cover the years 2000–2006, while providing adjustments to be made to take account of new countries joining the EU.

However, it should be noted that while both the European Parliament and the Commission are represented at meetings, the European Council is not an institution as such, and is therefore not subject to the controls which are imposed on the Council of the European Union.

THE EUROPEAN PARLIAMENT (EP)

Representing over 370 million people in the EU, and with 626 MEPs, the EP is the developed world's largest multinational parliament. Directly elected since 1979, prior to which its members were appointed by Member States, the EP has grown in size and influence, and now shares decision-making on certain matters with the Council of the EU. The number of MEPs a country sends is dependent on its size. Thus, Germany has the largest number of seats with 99, France, Italy and the UK have 87 each, Spain has 64, The Netherlands has 31, Belgium, Greece and Portugal have 25 each, Sweden has 22, Denmark and Finland have 16 each, Ireland has 15, and Luxembourg has six MEPs.

Originally set up as a supervisory body, with powers over the Budget, its role has increased steadily. To reduce what is perceived as the 'democratic deficit' of the EC, the Single European Act (SEA) gave it new powers by introducing a cooperation procedure in various areas where qualified majority voting is allowed. This was developed by the Treaty on European Union (TEU) which gave some co-decision powers with the Council, a negative assent procedure and greater rights to be consulted. The TEU also gave the EP the power to request the Commission to submit a proposal where the EP has decided by an absolute majority that new legislation is required. These rights are again being extended by the Amsterdam Treaty. Under the co-decision procedure, for certain areas set out in the TEU, the Council are obliged to work together with the EP to reach compromise agreements on proposals.

The supervisory powers of the EP remain, and they may exercise this in several ways – by way of written and oral questions, by discussion of the annual and other reports, by the discharge in respect of the implementation of the Budget (and prior agreement to it), through the motion of censure, and through the operation of the Parliamentary Ombudsman, who has wide powers of investigation. The motion of censure may only be used against the Commission and can only be carried by a two-thirds majority. The EP also has a role in the designation of the Commission and its President.

The office of Parliamentary Ombudsman was created by the TEU. Appointed by the EP, he can receive complaints from EU citizens, residents and companies relating to maladministration by any EU institution. The current Ombudsman is Jacob Magnus Soderman who will remain in office until the next EP elections in June 1999.

The Members of the European Parliament (MEPs) are elected every five years.

The EP generally holds a one-week part session every month except in August. There are also part sessions on specific topics: the budget, agricultural prices, etc. Plenary sessions are held in Strasbourg, although some committee meetings are now held in Brussels. Virtually all the MEPs are active in one of the 20 committees which cover the following areas of interest:

- Foreign affairs, security and defence
- Agriculture and rural developments
- Budgets
- Economic and monetary affairs
- Research, technological development and energy
- External economic relations
- Legal affairs and citizens' rights
- Social affairs and employment
- Regional policy
- Transport and tourism
- Environment, public health and consumer protection
- Culture, youth, education and the media
- Development and cooperation
- Civil liberties and internal affairs
- Budgetary control
- Institutional affairs
- Fisheries
- Petitions
- Women's rights
- Rules of procedure.

When a Commission proposal is submitted to the EP *en route* to Council it is considered by one or more of these committees. Reports prepared by specialist committees are usually published and discussed by the political groups before they are debated and voted upon in plenary session, after which the opinions or decisions are forwarded to the Council and Commission.

The MEPs divide along political rather than national lines, and most belong to one of the EP's transnational political groups. Presently the main political group is the party of European Socialists.

THE COMMISSION OF THE EUROPEAN COMMUNITIES

The Commission of the European Communities, usually referred to as the European Commission, or simply the Commission, is composed of 20 Commissioners, including the President and two Vice-Presidents of the Commission. Two Commissioners come from each 'big' Member State and one from each of the smaller states (see attached list), and all are appointed for five-year terms, by mutual agreement between Member States, and have to be approved by the EP. Each Member State undertakes not to attempt to influence the Commissioners in the performance of their tasks. Although national governments try to secure particular areas of Community business for their appointees, as the Commissioner has the responsibility for shaping EC policy in that particular area, the allocation of portfolios is ultimately the decision of the President of the Commission, currently Jacques Santer.

The two Commissioners from the UK are Neil Kinnock and Sir Leon Brittan. Their appointment was agreed between the prime minister and the leader of the opposition of the day after consultation with other political leaders in the UK and elsewhere in the Community.

The Commissioners form a College and all 20 Commissioners have to agree that a proposal is appropriate before it can be submitted to Council. Each Commissioner has his own 'Cabinet' or team of personal advisers whose functions are to keep the Commissioner fully briefed on all aspects of EC policy – ie not just his own portfolio – and to act as a think tank, initiating, refining and developing aspects of strategic policy in their Commissioner's particular area of responsibility.

The Commission is served by a staff of about 17 000, not including consultants. About 750 temporaries and 1600 of the staff are involved in translating activities, and it is this body which we usually think of when referring to the Commission (ie information can be obtained from the Commission....), and is divided into Directorates General.

A list of the Commissioners and Directorates General is set out on page 125.

The tasks of the European Commission are listed in Article 155 of the Treaty of Rome 1957, albeit they have been expanded since then as the competences of the Community have grown. The main powers of the Commission remain those of initiative, supervision and implementation. The Commission is largely based in Brussels, but has offices in Luxembourg, representation and information offices in each of the Member States, including offices in such places in the UK for example, as London, Cardiff, Edinburgh and Belfast, and has delegations in many of the world's capitals. It is interesting to note that a citizen of the EU can get protection from the consular or diplomatic authorities of any Member State if he or she is in a third country where his or her own national country is not represented.

The Commission's activity is centred mainly on its right, and indeed duty, to draft measures to be presented to the Council, and to ensure they are implemented. This is why the Commission is often described as the 'driving force' of the EC. The Commission, in making a proposal, needs to be acutely aware of the range of national and sectoral opinions and the likelihood of Member States accepting it. The Commission is obliged to seek the opinion of Member States before submitting proposals to the Council, and this has been outlined in what is referred to as the Luxembourg Compromise of 29 January 1966. This states that 'before adopting any particular important proposal, it is desirable that the Commission should establish appropriate contacts with the governments of the Member States without this procedure compromising the right of initiative which the Commission derives from the Treaty'. It is important to note that although the Commission is the starting point for Community action, it is not free to choose its own activities. It is obliged to act if the Community interest so requires. It is also limited by the guidelines agreed by the European Council in December 1992 on the principle of subsidiarity which followed the Treaty on European Union (TEU) provision that subsidiarity should limit EU action to those areas where it is more effective for Community action to be taken, rather than that national provision by Member States be made. This has been further refined to mean that decisions should be devolved to the lowest appropriate level, and in June

1998 the European Council decided that there should be a review of how this principle works in practice.

The Commission is empowered to administer the various funds of the EU, for example the European Agricultural Guidance and Guarantee Fund (EAGGF) for the operation of the Common Agricultural Policy (CAP). It is responsible for drawing up the draft budget of the EU and for directing investment to different parts of the EU through funds such as the European Social Fund (ESF) and the European Regional Development Fund (ERDF).

Although international agreements are concluded by the Council, they are first negotiated by the Commission, though under strict instructions from the Council. It is therefore the Commission which represents the Member States for example in the trade negotiations at the World Trade Organization.

The Commission is also responsible for implementation of EC policies once they have been approved by the Member States. In the agricultural sector for example, it seeks to manage the overall market by a series of measures (see Part V). It also has investigative and punitive powers in order to ensure implementation of Community measures – such as competition rules, with recourse to the European Court of Justice (ECJ). Thus, if the Community legislation is not complied with, the Commission may take individuals, companies, enterprises or even Member States before the ECJ. In 1996 the Commission started infringement proceedings in 1113 cases, although many were settled before reaching court (634). In 1997 the number of infringement cases started rose to 1436; and those resolved without referral to the ECJ rose to 1468. Since the TEU, the Commission has been able to request penalty payments to be provided for where a Member State fails to comply with an ECJ judgment, and the Commission has used these powers. One case involved penalty payments of £179,150 per day.

Closely linked to its role as guardian of the Treaties is the Commission's task of defending Community interests. As a matter of principle each Commissioner must serve no interests other than those of the EC, and must constantly strive to ensure that the Community interest prevails. He will therefore have to seek compromise solutions that take account of that interest. As a result, the Commission plays a vitally important role in mediating between the Member States.

The Directorates General (DGs) are similar to the various departments which make up a national civil service, but have additional translation services. The staff of the Commission are recruited proportionally from all

Member States although some Member States (eg the UK) tend to be under-represented, and applicants have to go through a fairly rigorous recruitment process. Once appointed, they must work in the interest of the EC as a whole, and not for their national or individual agenda. However, the rough balance of nationalities which is preserved in Brussels does help to avoid external or government pressures.

Another duty of the Commission is to try to keep the EU moving forward towards its various goals. Towards the end of each year the Commission agrees and makes public its plan for the year ahead, with a detailed work programme giving advance notice of what it hopes to achieve. It is regularly updated in the 'state of the Community' speech by the Commission President, and progress made is recorded in a series of monthly and annual reports and a variety of detailed documents. However, the Commission's action plan is only a programme of work, and only the Council can transform this into legislation. The considerable process of consultation and preparation which takes place before a policy proposal reaches the first published draft is described below. Once a piece of suggested legislation has been prepared, it is the duty of the responsible Commissioner to present it to his or her colleagues. It must be examined by all of them, and adopted if necessary by a majority vote, before being delivered formally to the Council and the EP. Appropriate agreement must be reached by the Council and possibly the EP before the proposal can become EC legislation. The proposal will then be published in the *Official Journal of the Community* as a draft Regulation (confusingly called a 'Decision' in the case of the ECSC) or a Directive.

THE COURT OF JUSTICE (ECJ)

The ECJ was set up under the Rome Treaty, and only has jurisdiction to rule on Community legislation. Its duty, as set down in the Treaty of Rome, Article 164 is to 'ensure that in the interpretation and application of the Treaty the law is observed'. There are six major areas of responsibility of the ECJ:

1. to rule in disputes between Member States
2. to rule in disputes between the EC and Member States
3. to rule in disputes between the institutions
4. to rule in disputes between individuals and the Community
5. to give opinions on international agreements

6. to give preliminary rulings, ie when disputes pending before national
   courts are referred by the latter to the ECJ.

The Court is composed of 15 judges and 9 advocates general to assist them.
The duty of the advocates general is to investigate cases with complete
impartiality and independence and submit their findings to the Court. The
judges and advocates general are appointed by common agreement of the
governments of the Member States for a six-year term of office. There is a
judge from each Member State. The judges elect the President of the Court
from among their number for a three-year term of office.

The ECJ has been an important institution in the development and interpretation of the Treaties and EC legislation. It has been invaluable in that
many of the restrictions introduced by the provisions were difficult for
some governments and large industries to accept and implement, particularly in the area of competition law or provisions to ensure free movement
of goods. The first actions to reach the ECJ almost all concerned these
issues, and most still do, but other problems have surfaced in the employment law sector, and enforcement of equal opportunities directives for
example, and in environmental provisions. Thus, for example, the UK was
taken to the Court over breaches of the failure to meet EC environmental
standards on some UK beaches in 1990.

When Community legislation has been passed, it becomes part of
national law, and it is then the duty of the governments of Member States to
ensure that the law is not only properly implemented, but also enforced.
Sometimes it is not companies that breach the rules, but the governments
themselves that fail to implement provisions properly, or try to evade them
for various reasons. Thus the Commission's first task is to seek to establish
the facts of the case and establish whether the breach is accidental, or an
oversight, or cynical. Normally the Commission will give the offending
government a reasonable time to offer an explanation, and only if this is not
forthcoming or is not convincing will the Commission refer the matter to
the ECJ. If a government is found guilty, the Commission will first exert
pressure to achieve compliance, and if this does not work, since the TEU
the Court can consider requests from the Commission to fine countries
which continue to infringe. The power to fine enterprises for breach of the
provisions is not so new, however, and has often been used to fine them for
breaches of Community legislation – most notoriously for breaches of
competition provisions.

Private individuals, firms, local authorities or others may appeal to the
ECJ when they feel they have been unjustly treated by Community legisla-

tion. There are no court costs involved, although appellants must brief counsel and pay their own legal fees. In the case of a private person who feels that he or she has been affected adversely by Community legislation, the first step is to complain to the Commission, a simple procedure which can be initiated by a letter to any of the Commission offices.

A Court of First Instance was set up following a recommendation by the ECJ in 1987 to take some of the case load. Its purpose was to determine in the first instance certain classes of action or proceeding brought by natural or legal persons, subject to appeal to the ECJ. However, it is not competent to deal with actions brought by Member States. Since 1994 it has also assumed jurisdiction in dumping and subsidy cases.

Judgments of the Court are available for consultation in Commission Offices. Advice on the role of the Court and how to approach it can also be offered by the European Lawyers' Groups in England, Wales, Scotland and Northern Ireland.

THE COURT OF AUDITORS

Before 1977 the European Community was audited by an audit board set up under Article 206 of the Treaty of Rome, Article 180 of the EURATOM Treaty, and Article 78d of the ECSC Treaty. However, the Community's financial autonomy and the expansion of the EC budget made it necessary to set up an independent Court of Auditors enjoying wider powers of control.

The European Court of Auditors was set up by the Treaty of Brussels of 22 July 1975 which entered into force in July 1977. It assists the EP and the Council in exercising their powers of control over the implementation of the Community budget.

The importance of the Court of Auditors, particularly given the increase in the incidence of fraud concerning Community funds, was recognized in the TEU which made it an institution in its own right. It therefore became the fifth Community institution, alongside the Council, EP, Commission and Court of Justice.

The Court of Auditors has 15 members, appointed for a six-year term, most of whom have experience in their own national audit bodies. The Court examines the accounts of all revenue and expenditure of the Community, and of all bodies set up by the EC. The Court's role is to examine whether all revenue has been received and all expenditure incurred in a lawful and regular manner, and whether the financial management has been sound. The audit is based on records and, if necessary, performed on the spot in the institutions of the EU and in the Member States in collaboration with the national audit bodies. All information pertaining to the Court's audit must be made freely available.

At the end of the financial year, the Court draws up an annual report on the management of the ECSC and the other instruments of Community policy. The Court may also, at any time, submit observations on specific questions and deliver opinions at the request of any of the Community institutions, on its own initiative. Special reports of the Court have included investigations of the policy for distillation measures in the table wine sector, food aid supplied to India, the export refunds policy, and the operation of the ERDF. More recent reports include a highly critical investigation into the Community's tourism policy in which the Court deplored the lack of transparency in selecting projects to be funded and inadequate financial and project monitoring. The Court was equally critical in its investigations into programmes for non-EU Mediterranean countries, and the operation of the Common Agricultural Policy (CAP).

The Court's reports and opinions are examined by the Council and the EP. The Commission is forced to remedy those complaints to which the Court has drawn attention, and which have been endorsed by the EP.

THE COMMITTEE OF PERMANENT REPRESENTATIVES (COREPER)

The decision-making process does not only involve the Commission, the Council and the EP. As often as possible, agreement on EC policies is reached at the level of COREPER, the Committee of Permanent Representatives. These are normally individuals of ambassadorial status representing and appointed by each Member State. COREPER is the administrative arm of the Council. Any agreements at their level would usually be formally ratified by national ministers in council as 'A' or Agreed points.

When COREPER cannot agree proposals, then they come to the Council for debate. For example agricultural matters are dealt with by a council involving agriculture ministers, transport matters are for transport ministers, and so on. The Council can invite the Commission to redraft proposals, summon expert help and occasionally make tense and prolonged calls to seek national approvals for their stances. These meetings are held frequently.

The Council proper – consisting of Foreign Ministers – meets to provide top-level guidance, review progress and keep targets firmly in mind. The Prime Ministers only come into the act as a kind of last resort, or through the European Council.

ECONOMIC AND SOCIAL COMMITTEE (ESC OR ECOSOC) (AND THE EUROPEAN COAL AND STEEL CONSULTATIVE COMMITTEE)

By analogy with similar national institutions, the ECSC, the EEC and EURATOM were provided with advisory bodies consisting of representatives of various action groups. The role of these bodies in the activities of the EU is threefold:

- They assist the process of shared decision-making by communicating to the Commission and Council their opinion as to various actual or projected legislation, together with advice as to where priorities should lie as to objectives.
- They provide a permanent and favoured forum for economic and social dialogue and consultation between their individual member groups.
- They form an essential channel of information to professional circles and the public at large on community matters.
- Thus they provide an essential role in the process of integration.

In the area covered by the ECSC, this function is performed by the Consultative Committee. This Committee currently consists of 96 members comprising equal representation from producers, consumers, workers and dealers from the coal and steel industries.

The ESC comprises 222 members (France, Germany, Italy and the UK with 24 each; Spain 21; Austria, Belgium, The Netherlands, Greece, Portugal and Sweden with 12; Denmark, Finland and Ireland with 9; Luxembourg 6). The composition of the Committee must represent various categories of economic and social activity, and include one-third of the seats for employers, one-third for employees, and one-third for other categories – consumers, dealers, etc.

The members are appointed by the Council on the basis of proposals from the national governments. The full ESC meets in Brussels ten times a year, and adopts some 180 opinions each year, of which around 20 are on its own initiative. These opinions may be found in the *Official Journal of the European Communities* 'C' series.

The ESC, while purely consultative (so that its opinions are not binding on the Community institutions), is very influential. Perhaps most notably in 1989 its opinion on fundamental social rights formed the basis of the subsequent Social Charter (see Chapter III).

The ESC works closely with the EP, and both formal and informal contacts have grown up between them. In 1981 the EP made a resolution which provided specifically for information exchanges. The members of the Committee of the Regions are also now becoming involved in joint contacts.

THE COMMITTEE OF THE REGIONS

One of the EU's newest advisory bodies, the Committee of the Regions, was established by the TEU to represent the views of the local and regional authorities in the EU decision-making process. Local government had lobbied strongly for such formal consultation on the grounds that it was involved in implementing and enforcing much EU legislation, and represented the level of government closest to the people. Thus the Committee must be consulted on a number of areas set out in the TEU, and these include TENs (Trans-European networks in transport, energy and communications), education and youth, culture, public health, and economic and social cohesion. It should be noted that increasingly it is being consulted on other matters too, and is able to issue opinions on most matters where regional issues or interests are at stake, on its own initiative as well as following consultation. However, like the ESC, its position is purely advisory, and the institutions are under no obligation to act on its recommendations. Like its sister body, the ESC, the Committee of the Regions has 222 full members (plus 222 substitutes). The numbers of representatives are as follows:

- France, Germany, Italy and the UK   24
- Spain   21
- Austria, Belgium, Greece, The Netherlands   12
  Portugal and Sweden
- Denmark, Finland and Ireland   9
- Luxembourg   6

Members are appointed for four years on the nominations from Member States. Membership of the Committee is diverse, and ranges from Councillors from small English districts to Presidents of the mighty German Länder. There is no legal requirement for equal representations between levels of local government, prompting heated debate in several countries between regional and local tiers as to who should sit on the Committee.

The Committee meets in plenary session every two to three months to adopt Opinions prepared by its eight sub-committees (confusingly known as 'Commissions'. Meetings take place in the European Parliament's building in Brussels.

THE EUROPEAN INVESTMENT BANK

This was set up in 1958 under the Treaty of Rome as the banking institution of the European Communities for long-term project finance. Its shareholders are the member states of the EU. It should be distinguished from, and not confused with, the European Central Bank (ECB).

THE EUROPEAN CENTRAL BANK (ECB) AND EUROPEAN MONETARY INSTITUTE (EMI)

The ECB will become fully operational and takes over from the EMI, which has had the task of preparing for the single currency, on 1 January 1999. Mr Wim Duisenberg of the Netherlands Central Bank is its first President, and may step down after four years of his eight-year term, in favour of Jean Claude Trichet of France's Central Bank for the remainder of that term.

The ECB will be responsible for coordinating the Central Banks of Member States, of maintaining currency price stability, and managing the Euro and other monetary matters arising from Economic and Monetary Union (EMU). See also Part IV.

OTHER BODIES AND INSTITUTIONS

There are many other bodies and institutions which are set up by or allied to the EC for various purposes, some to assist in the consultation process, some to assist in implementation of provisions. Many of them will be listed as useful addresses at the end of this book. Examples include the European

Consumers Consultative Committee, the European Centre for the Development of Vocational Training, the Foundation for the Improvement of Living and Working Conditions, the European Environment Agency, the European Assembly for Science and Technology, the Office for Veterinary and Plant Inspection and Control, the European Monitoring Centre for Drugs and Drug Addiction, the European Police Office (EUROPOL), the Agency for Health and Safety at Work and the European Commission Information Users Committee; and the European Medicines Evaluation Agency which is situated in London.

Part III

From the Treaty of Rome to the Single Market and European Union

FROM FREE TRADE TO A SINGLE MARKET

The objective of creating a common market within the EC was enshrined in the Treaty of Rome. This reflected the Community's aim of achieving free trade and free competition. In 1957 the first goal pursued was to create a genuine common market by establishing a customs union within the Community, so between 1958 and 1969 quotas and customs duties restricting trade between the original six members of the Community were abolished. As the Community was enlarged, so these arrangements were also applied to the new members. At the same time the Community also established a Common Customs Tariff (CCT) which was applied to goods imported into any Member State from countries outside the Community.

In addition to quantitative barriers to trade within the Community, there were also hundreds of physical, technical and fiscal barriers. These obstacles included varying national technical specifications, health and safety standards, environmental regulations, quality controls and differences in VAT between Member States. At the beginning of the 1980s, although the Community had had some success in removing some of these barriers, a true common market did not yet exist. The tension between the requirements inherent in establishing and maintaining the smooth running of the Common Market, on the one hand, and national interests, on the other, had led to paralysis. The Treaty of Rome had failed to ensure the consistency needed in the economic integration process between the abolition of national barriers in order to create a Single Market, and the implementation of a common policy or a policy coordinated by the Community.

Since 1957 the Community of 6 has expanded several times – from 6 to 9 in 1973, to 10 in 1981, to 12 in 1986 and to 15 in 1995 – and there are preparations in hand to admit even more members. These successive enlargements presented the Community with further challenges in trying to integrate the Community markets, and indeed with the signature of the European Economic Area agreement in 1992, with the extra EFTA countries included in that. During the same period the EC had to face oil price shocks and the effects of global economic recession. Throughout all this, the EC had lost out competitively to the USA and Japan. The incomplete integration of the European economy combined with fiercer international competition reinforced the view that the economic policies of the Member States of the EC needed to be coordinated more closely. Thus, in 1985 a White Paper was adopted that traced the consequences of the removal of non-tariff barriers, the action that would be required to ensure that the removal of the different barriers worked in a coordinated way, and the timetable which laid out stages for achieving a frontier-free Single Market by:

1. removing physical barriers (frontier controls, transport quotas, etc)
2. the abolition of technical barriers to trade and the prevention of new ones, together with more freedom for workers and professionals, a common market for services, including financial institutions, freer capital movement and more industrial cooperation
3. the removal of fiscal barriers, by bringing VAT rates closer together and tackling problems of excise duties (as distinct from customs duties).

The Single European Act (SEA) 1986, while formally endorsing these objectives, also provided the appropriate legal framework for completion of the Single Market. The SEA was ratified by all the Member States, and came into force on 1 July 1997.
The 1988 Cecchini Report had outlined the costs of not achieving a Single Market and can be summed up as follows:

- high administrative costs incurred in dealing with different bureaucratic requirements
- higher transport costs because of border formalities
- increased costs as a result of compliance with different national standards, and therefore smaller production runs
- duplication of costs involved in separate research and development
- high costs of non-competitive and heavily regulated state activities, as exemplified by national public procurement policies

- high costs and reduced choice for the consumer confined to his national market
- the opportunity costs which prevent or at best discourage economic activity from spreading across frontiers to enjoy the full market potential.

The 1996 survey over two years of the operation of the Single Market, and the subsequent report by the Commission gave a positive result for the Single Market, but reported that some of the trade obstacles noted in the Cecchini Report still remained. Much has been done since, however, and now the impetus centres on supporting innovation, increasing competitiveness, and creating jobs in the EU, besides making EMU work – all of which require greater cooperation between Member States. It is therefore expected that remaining barriers to inter-EU trade will crumble. Some 282 legislative proposals had been put forward in order to create the Single Market in the Community by 1992. By March 1997, 273 of these were in force throughout the EU. There has often been considerable debate over the correct implementation of some of these measures, and compromise solutions have been sought. The situations of VAT and excise duties provide useful examples, as despite some harmonization, and for VAT agreed minimum rates, wide variations still occur to take account of national sensitivities – eg zero rates for food and children's clothing in the UK.

Where new national provisions that might create barriers to trade are proposed, they have to be scrutinized after notification to the Commission to ensure their compliance with Single Market principles. Community-proposed legislation first has to jump various hurdles. It has to comply with subsidiarity and environmental guidelines, and be subjected to compliance costs tests before being put forward for approval.

It is interesting to note that a large proportion of the Single Market provisions, often called the 1992 programme as they were set out in the White Paper which set out the programme leading to the Single Market and the SEA 1986, related to veterinary and phytosanitary controls. The provisions which cause the most problems in respect of implementation are those (perhaps not surprisingly) dealing with public procurement, which is now also subject to World Trade Organization (WTO) rules; and competition provisions, for example preventing unfair state aids. In this area too, the WTO provisions and disparate resolution procedures are gaining in importance.

THE SINGLE EUROPEAN ACT (SEA) 1986

The SEA reformed the Treaty of Rome on which the European Communities were based, with the purpose of accelerating European integration through improvements in the functioning of the institutions (widening of powers) and greater speed and flexibility in the decision-making process. The Single European Act therefore provided the legal framework and the 31 December 1992 deadline for completion of the Internal Market.

Almost all the proposals in the previous White Paper on the removal of physical, technical and fiscal barriers to create the Single Market would have had to have been adopted unanimously by all the Member States had the SEA not entered into force, but the Act extended the rule on qualified majority voting (QMV) within the Council to a very large number of decisions relating to the Internal Market so that a single country could not block progress in what were seen as Single Market matters. Thus, QMV was extended to:

- all types of autonomous modification or suspension of the duties applicable under the common customs tariff
- measures on the protection of savings and the exercise of medical, para-medical and pharmaceutical professions
- the freedom to provide services
- the free movement of capital
- the common policy on sea and air transport
- the approximation of national legislation aimed at completing the internal market with the exception of taxation, freedom of movement for persons, and measures concerning the rights and interests of employed persons for which unanimity was still required.

The last provision (Article 100A of the Treaty) was seen as the key to the completion of the internal market. However, it had two weak points. First, it gave rise to difficulties of interpretation because of the derogation for major needs referred to in Article 36 of the Treaty (restrictions on imports justified mainly on grounds of security and public health) or relating to protection of the environment or the working environment. Second, it excluded fiscal provisions, which were particularly important in the White Paper programme, because the SEA retained the rule of unanimity in the new Article 99 of the Treaty (which concerned taxation).

Another essential innovation which the SEA introduced was in the decision-making process – to apply the cooperation procedure to decisions to be taken by QMV and to strengthen the EP's legislative powers by introducing the possibility of amending texts. The SEA also gave the Commission more powers in the implementation of measures adopted by the Council of Ministers.

As there was concern that the Single Market would put grave stresses on the economies of the weaker Member States, the SEA extended the scope of the Treaty to include new common policies. Because vigorous monetary, regional, social, budgetary, technology and competition policies had to be implemented quickly, two inter-governmental conferences (IGCs) were set up to run in parallel, and these resulted in the Treaty on European Union signed at Maastricht.

THE TREATY ON EUROPEAN UNION 1992 (TEU)

Thus the Treaty on European Union 1992 (often referred to as the TEU, or the Union Treaty, or the Maastricht Treaty after the place of signature) was the result of the two inter-governmental conferences (IGCs) which concluded in 1991. It was finally ratified by all Member States by November 1993, when it came into force. It has had a significant impact, building on the framework principle laid by the Treaty of Rome, that there should be incremental steps towards 'an ever closer union of the peoples of Europe', and on the developments agreed in the SEA. The main aims of the TEU were:

- to promote economic and social progress in the EU through the creation of a single market without frontiers through the strengthening of economic and social cohesion and through the introduction of Economic and Monetary Union (EMU)
- to assert the European identity on the international scene, particularly through the implementation of a common foreign and defence policy
- to protect the interests of the nationals of Member States through the introduction of European citizenship
- to develop close cooperation between the Member States on justice and home affairs
- to ensure the effectiveness of the mechanisms and institutions of the Community.

To strengthen the Union of Member States, the Treaty was structured so as to stand the European 'house' on three pillars. The first pillar embraced all the existing policies under the previous treaties which continued under the Community umbrella. The second introduced a section on Common Foreign and Security Policy (CFSP) and took into account the possibility of a common defence policy in the future. It was not under the European Communities' jurisdiction, but introduced new areas of cooperation between the Member States, as did the third pillar that related to matters of justice and home affairs, including police and judicial matters. It should be noted that in both the second and third pillars the Council had to act unanimously, the EP only had a consultative role, and the jurisdiction of the ECJ was limited.

Importantly, it enabled the extension of Community competence to new policy areas where this was seen to be needed, and gave the institutions a more active role in setting up TENs, in environmental protection, research and development and industrial policy among others, and reinforced the powers of the European Parliament. It also provided for a cohesion fund to assist with economic and social progress and the improvement of the quality of life in the EU.

Like the earlier SEA, the TEU comprised amendments to the Treaty of Rome.

Thus, the new aspects of the TEU following on from its objectives were:

1. to establish a single currency in the context of Economic and Monetary Union (EMU) by 1999 at the latest; and to ensure cohesion of the economies of the Member States for this
2. to establish new rights for citizens of the Member States of the EU as citizens of the EU
3. to extend the Community's field of responsibility in the following areas: consumer protection, public health, visas, the creation of major transport, telecommunications and energy infrastructures, namely Trans-European Networks (TENs), industrial policy, education, culture, environmental protection, research and development and social policy (albeit the UK then had an opt out) and cooperation on anti-crime policies
4. to extend the powers of the European Parliament in EC decision-making, the appointment of the Commission and in external relations policy
5. to introduce a Common Foreign and Security Policy (CFSP).

Economic and Monetary Union (EMU) has been the most discussed area of the TEU, and is also dealt with elsewhere in this book. However, it is useful to remember that EMU means that the currencies of the participating Member States are locked irrevocably to one another at the same exchange rate. This prevents any devaluations of individual currencies from taking place, and means that individual countries cannot use this method to control their economies. The economic policies of Member States participating in EMU have to be co-ordinated, particularly with regard to inflation and national debt. It is assumed that EMU will improve prospects for growth as a result of stable prices, transparency, and the absence of currency conversion costs.

The agreement on EMU at Maastricht set the structure, goals and timetable for achieving a high degree of economic convergence between Member States, and the creation of a single currency, the Euro, and it has now been agreed that the Member States who have complied (some would say that a little bit of cheating has been going on) with the convergence criteria will be part of the Single Currency as of 1 January 1999. Eleven Member States are scheduled to be participants –ie all the Member States except the UK and Denmark (which both had opt outs under the Treaty and had decided not to join at this time but may decide to join later); and Greece and Sweden, neither of which have met the criteria.

On 1 January 1999 the European Central Bank (ECB) will replace the EMI, take over the management of the currency reserves of participating Member States and manage the currency; and will deal with the single monetary policy. All this is now settled.

The problems raised by economic and social cohesion in the EU in practice have meant that the richer and more developed countries have had to shoulder more of the burden of structural adjustment in the Community's less advantaged regions. This issue had been addressed in the SEA and contributions and funds had been increased and reorganized, and the system has worked well. However, similar problems are now having to be considered with regard to the new applicants for EU membership, and the costs to existing members that efforts to prepare their economies for the extra strains of joining the EU will bring, and this is likely to cause problems in the contributing countries.

The TEU covered a range of domestic issues affecting the future development of the EU. It defined priorities for making EU industry more competitive. Considerable emphasis was put on supporting Research and Development (R&D) in new technologies and in helping to meet industry's needs by training programmes to create a better qualified workforce. Specific programmes were drawn up for particular sectors.

Education policy featured highly in the Treaty, with several objectives outlined, in particular increasing the teaching and dissemination of languages of the Member States, to encourage the mobility of students and teachers and the academic recognition of diplomas and periods of study; and to promote cooperation between educational establishments. Much has been done since the TEU in this area.

Extending the EU's powers over social policy legislation proved to be one of the most divisive issues at Maastricht. The argument for this legislation was that it would provide the necessary protection for workers when the competitive pressures began to bite. The UK was alone in its opposition to moves to encourage EU-wide legislation on improved living and working conditions, terms of employment, employee consultation and social security issues. It was therefore agreed to include a protocol to the Treaty whereby the provisions of the Social Chapter, as it was called, would not apply in the UK. It should be noted that the UK has now ended its opt out of the Social Chapter, and therefore participates fully both in discussions and implementation of provisions.

The TEU made provisions for the establishment of a Common Foreign and Security Policy for the EU, which was seen to be of vital importance in the context of economic union and the position of the EU internationally. These provisions have to be considered in the light of the existing CFSP process, the Organization for Security and Cooperation in Europe (OSCE) and Western European Union (WEU) which is likely to become the defence arm of the EU in the future. The agreement at Maastricht enabled the Member States to arrive at common positions in these matters, albeit they could still exercise their right of veto on important questions of collective action. It should be noted that the Amsterdam Treaty has carried this much further as the TEU provisions were not felt to go far enough, although the Treaty still allows for a system of constructive abstention.

There was a clear realization that relaxing the internal Community frontiers in the drive to achieve the Single Market with a frontier-free zone had made cross-border cooperation imperative to tackle a possible growth in organized international crime. Another factor was the spectre of waves of immigrants entering the EU from Southern and Eastern Europe. The TEU therefore covered areas where inter-governmental cooperation was necessary, ie to fight illegal drugs, fraud, terrorism, and illegal trafficking in women and children.

The whole issue of subsidiarity – ie the extent to which the Community institutions should intervene or legislate in the economic, financial, social and political development of the EU – was also discussed at length at Maastricht, with different states viewing it in different ways. For example the UK saw subsidiarity as a means of curbing Brussels' excesses, whereas Germany viewed it as a means of preserving the delicate balance between local communities, the regional state and federal levels of government. The TEU defined the principle in the following way:

> In arenas which do not fall within its exclusive competence, the Community shall take action, in accordance with the principle of subsidiarity, only if and in so far as the objectives of the proposed action cannot be sufficiently achieved by Member States, and can therefore, by reason of the scale of the effects of the proposed action, be better achieved by the Community. Any action by the Community shall not go beyond what is necessary to achieve the objectives of the Treaty.

As part of the drive to bring legislation closer to the people, the TEU set out guidelines for the creation of a Committee of the Regions (CoR) which is described elsewhere in this book (see page 11). The TEU also addressed the overall decision-making structure of the EC, and extended the powers of the EP (see page 14).

THE TREATY FOR EUROPE (THE AMSTERDAM TREATY) 1997

This Treaty was signed in October 1997 in Amsterdam following the IGC and is, at the time of writing well on its way to ratification by all the Member States. It builds on the second and third pillars of the TEU, but although it was intended originally to deal with institutional problems to prepare the EU for expansion to absorb the new applicants, in fact the emphasis was on tackling unemployment, although some important amendments were made. Thus, the Amsterdam Treaty emphasizes the need for Member States to work together in economic policies to stimulate growth and create jobs. It streamlines voting procedures and the qualified majority voting areas that will include some areas currently subject to unanimity, such as rights of establishment and research aid. The powers of the EP are extended, and the co-decision procedure will be extended (so that the EP will adopt provisions jointly with Council, or reject proposals) in areas such as Trans European Networks (TENs) and employment policy. The principle of subsidiarity is further defined and limited. The Justice and Home Affairs area of cooperation is to be gradually brought under Community competence, and the Schengen Acquis on the abolition of border controls, although subject to special provisions for the UK, Ireland and the Nordic countries, protecting the Nordic Passport Union and enabling the UK and Ireland to continue their common travel area, and retain frontier controls, is integrated into the framework of the EU. The Amsterdam Treaty also includes a Charter of Human Rights, and sanctions for abuse of human rights will be imposable on Member States breaching its principles. The Social Charter was incorporated into the Treaty, and this effectively ends the UK opt out and as noted above, it now participates in provisions agreed on, and discussions in this area.

Although it has been the subject of rather a low profile, being overshadowed by the debate and progress towards EMU, in fact the Amsterdam Treaty will have some significant effects, and merits careful reading. For example it apparently resolves the debate about whether individual Member States can proceed more quickly towards closer union if they wish to do so – by stating that they may do so, provided that the interests of non-participating Member States are protected.

As to the development of the EU – it is changing all the time – and developing as the need arises. Account has to be taken of developments on the world stage, in the context of global trade agreements made under the umbrella of the World Trade Organization, which covers some 80 per cent of world trade with over 120 participating countries.

EMU will have a huge impact, and the expansion of the EU will necessitate further changes – most obviously in institutional matters and in terms of decision-making, but also in respect of agricultural policy. One might almost say: 'Watch this space'.

Much has been written about the Treaty of Rome, and more recently, the SEA, the TEU and indeed the Amsterdam Treaty. The Commission and the European Parliament have, of course, produced useful booklets, and information is available on their website. A most useful Progress Report from the European Commission presented by Mario Monti (the Commissioner in charge of the Single Market) entitled *The Single Market and Tomorrow's Europe* (ISBN 0 7494 2266 1) published in 1996, gives an extremely useful overview, and is the result of considerable detailed research.

Part IV

Decision-making and how it is influenced

THE DIFFERENT FORMS OF COMMUNITY PROVISIONS

There are various types of Community legal instrument, and it is important to understand the differences between them. There are:

- regulations: once adopted by Council a regulation is binding in its entirety and applicable as it stands in all Member States, either immediately, or on the implementation dates agreed. Regulations are therefore comparable to national law. Sometimes eg under Competition articles of the Treaties, the Commission can issue regulations.
- Directives: a Directive is different from a regulation in that, although binding on the Member States on the results to be achieved, the form and method of achieving these results are left to the discretion of the national authorities. However, if a Directive is sufficiently detailed and clear, it may be considered effective before actual implementation, after the due implementation date, even if the Member State has failed to implement it, or failed to implement it by the due date.
- decisions: a decision is similar to a regulation in that it is binding on those to whom it is addressed, although it is usually addressed to one or more Member States, or indeed an enterprise.
- recommendations or opinions: these are not legally binding, unlike regulations, Directives and decisions, and constitute advice, albeit with political impact, to governments.
- a notice: this is not legislation as such, but provides guidance.

WHO TAKES THE DECISIONS CONCERNING LEGISLATION?

The Council takes the Community's decisions acting on proposals submitted by the Commission, and the EP has the right of co-decision in some areas. Proposals may be far-reaching or very specific.

On most occasions national ministers have before them detailed reports and opinions from the EP and the ECOSOC and the Committee of the Regions to help them in their deliberations. Other 'easier' points on the agenda are usually agreed at a lower level.

If proposed legislation is particularly difficult, and individual Councils of junior Ministers cannot reach agreement, the legislation may be passed up to the Council at Foreign Minister level, which meets several times a year. If agreement cannot be reached there, it must be considered by the European Council – the 'Summit' which meets at least twice a year, and which is composed of Prime Ministers and Presidents plus the President of the Commission.

Decision-making can be based only on the Community treaties, and it is useful to distinguish between the legislative instruments described on page 37 and know the different legislative procedures that depend on the articles under which the proposals for legislation are brought; and to understand that the decisions of the ECJ interpret the treaties and the legislation made under them. It would, for example, be improper for the Council to rule that the death penalty should be introduced throughout the Community for terrorist assassinations, since no clause in the Treaties gives it power to act in such a matter of domestic criminal law. BUT it can agree (and has done so) on joint action to track down terrorists across frontiers, since this transnational action is permissible under the Treaties.

Decision-making is distinguished by the extraordinary information-gathering which takes place before a proposal even reaches the Council, and by its openness which can make disagreements between Ministers of Member States all too public. It is partly to avoid public conflicts that the IGCs are needed before changes to the Treaties.

Once a proposal is adopted by the Commission, it is then traditionally first considered by the Council in a *tour de table*. All 15 Member States say their piece, followed by debate. The President of the Council can exercise considerable influence: and remember that Member States assume the Presidency in turn every six months. Throughout the Council discussions, Commission and national experts are on hand to redraft proposals.

As noted above, depending on the matter under discussion, the Council may reach agreement by unanimity, or absolute or qualified majority vote. Council decisions are reached by a process of ongoing negotiation. The ECJ plays no direct part in the process. Its job is to rule on the fair and honest implementation of agreements once they are reached.

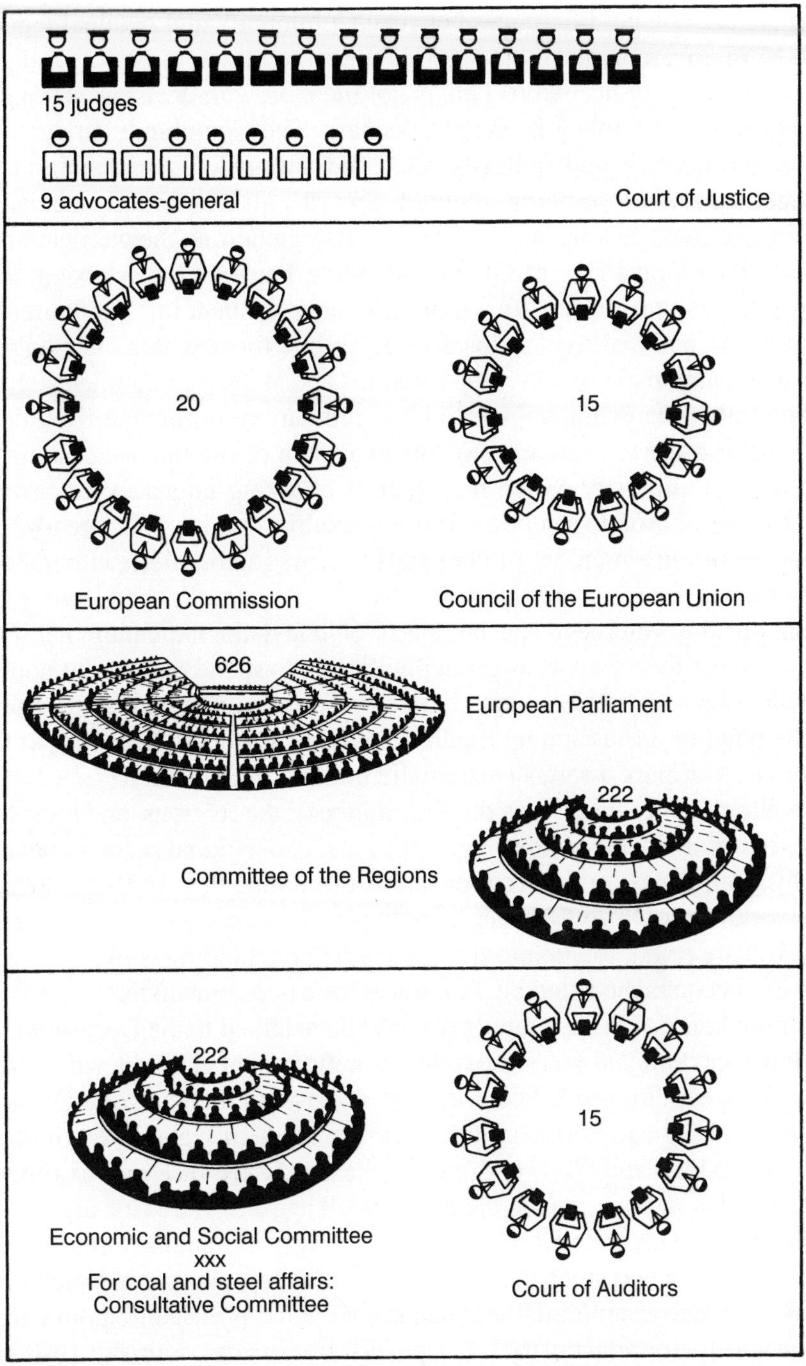

15 judges

9 advocates-general

Court of Justice

20

European Commission

15

Council of the European Union

626

European Parliament

Committee of the Regions

222

222

Economic and Social Committee
xxx
For coal and steel affairs:
Consultative Committee

15

Court of Auditors

Figure 2 The institutions of the European Community

There are crucial differences between Community and national legislation. Most governments of the world prepare their laws in secrecy, and present them as a *fait accompli*. This is not the case with decision-making in the EC where the policy is one of openness. The Community Budget, for example is publicly and endlessly discussed, savaged, restored and usually savaged again before being adopted. So with all Community decision-making. It involves long and detailed opinion gathering, the publication of an ever-changing string of Green and White Papers for discussion, and, above all, opportunities for lobbying and influencing the outcome unknown in national terms. However, it is up to those with a view on proposed legislation to use these opportunities and at the right moment.

The following example gives a clear indication of how the EC's decision-making works. You are, say, the chairman of the finance committee of a district authority which has been discharging unprocessed sewage into a river for around a century. It is not a subject which you care to think about too often; a member of your staff follows it, doubtless with no wild enthusiasm.

But one day you see a 'special report' on television indicating that if the Eurocrats get their way, your council will have to spend millions of pounds in building advanced treatment plants for sewerage. The whole question is on the point of discussion by Environmental Ministers in Brussels. At this point you compose a series of dramatic minutes and letters to your fellow councillors, representative on the Committee of the Regions, and local MP. You give un-attributable briefings to the local and national press, indicating the disaster ahead for your ratepayers if these meddlers in Brussels have their way. No doubt you will get some impressive reportage, but you are too late. You are trying to get into the game when the bidding is over, the contract has been reached, and the first tricks have been played to.

Within hours of the TV report you will have talked to the Department of the Environment, and read the wodge of government circulars which have been on its files for years. You will have discovered that there are Community rules, long ago agreed, on the degree to which we are permitted by international law to pollute bathing beaches, interfere with marine life and fishing rights or contaminate the high seas. The rules were first argued out in the 1970s in great detail by experts from every Community country and have been extended since then. Environmental groups gave extensive evidence. The European Parliament had prepared a report spelling out consequences for various industries, ratepayers, consumers, tourist boards and marine biologists. Other local authorities have built sewage treatment plants with the help of huge grants from the Community. After endless painful consultation the governments of all EC Members have come to conclusions on what their Environment Ministers plan to say about the implementation and possible extension of these agreements in the Council in Brussels. AND you are seriously hoping to change their stances now!...

THE VARIOUS STAGES

Although there are various procedures whereby legislation is passed (ie consultation, cooperation, co-decision and simplified co-decision and assent), the time to influence the Community's decision-making is as early as possible in the process, ideally at the consultation stages before a draft is produced – ie when discussions continue as to whether legislation in the area is necessary or appropriate, and cost compliance assessment audits are being carried out. There are four different stages, as follows:

- Stage 1: the Consultation stage: look out for the Green Papers which set out all the background and the general options; then watch for the White Papers which will set out the proposals for reform usually in quite specific terms, with a view to finding out the snags. At both these times the new proposal will be being considered by working groups and experts.
- Stage 2: when the first draft becomes public is also a good time to make detailed comments, as is
- Stage 3: when the draft is being considered by the EP and its Committees, and ECOSOC and possibly the CoR.
- Stage 4: when the revised draft is being considered again by the Commissioners and COREPER before being submitted to the Council.

It should be noted that there will probably be one official in the Commission with special responsibility for a particular topic (depending on its range and importance), and he will be eager to have well-informed comment. He will probably be receiving a very significant number of submissions from other Commission Directorates, besides national government departments and individuals, so it is wise to put a summary of important points on the first page. He will also be canvassing a large number of interested bodies, and many of these will be making submissions through their own government departments or international organizations, but there is nothing to prevent them from sending their comments directly to the Commission, and this is often encouraged, particularly at the early stages.

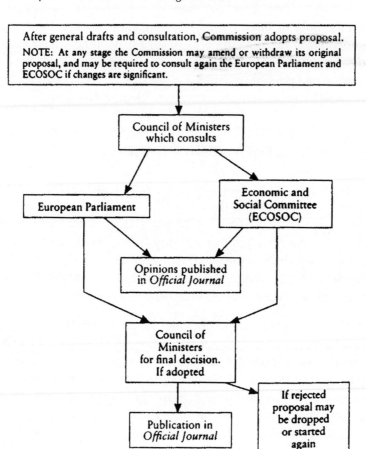

Figure 3 Consultation procedure

The official at the Commission will be coordinating the drafting of the proposal, and possibly coordinating the effort to achieve the necessary agreements between the Member States – at least as far as possible, before the proposal goes forward. Thus, Stage 1 is the time to speak up when you have something to say about proposed legislation, and when the Commission has an absolute duty to pay attention. But it is also true that the big guns will make the most noise. You will have to shout hard before anyone in Brussels hears you.

Fortunately it is the UK government's duty to sound out UK interests and make sure that the Directorates take them into account. The government will, therefore shout for you, and is good at it. Stage 1 is therefore the best time to tackle your local MP, write to government departments, speak

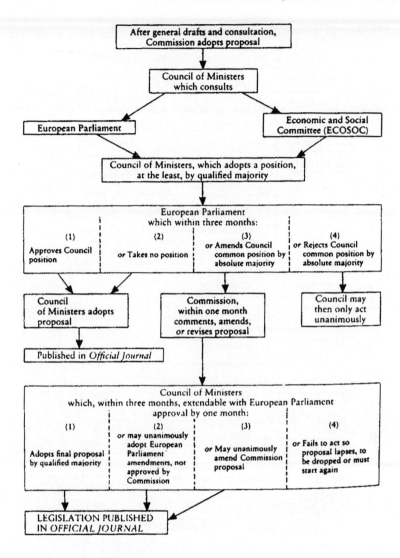

Figure 4 Co operation procedure

to the experts in the UK Permanent Representation, fire off letters to newspapers, and make sure that your comments are known to your professional, business and trade associations, and your MEP, and your representative on the Committee of the Regions. In short, this is the best time to lobby, as it easiest to change minds before positions become entrenched.

Stage 2 usually begins when the details of the new proposal are leaked to and then taken up by the press – usually partially referred to, often

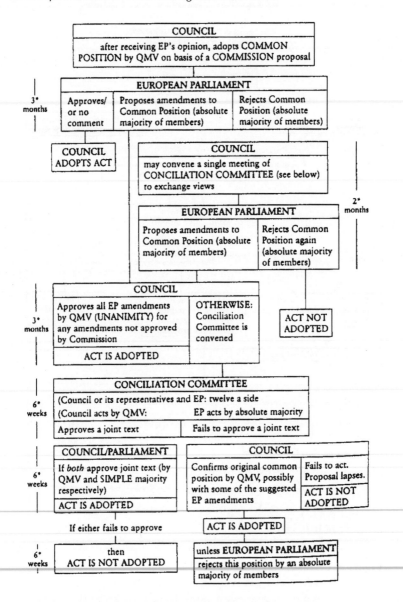

*These periods may be extended by one month or two weeks.

Figure 5   The co-decision procedure.

Source: House of Commons, Foreign Affairs Committee, Europe after Maastricht, vol. II, London 1992, p.9.

dishonestly and sometimes spectacularly. This 'panic publicity' is one of the aspects of the very open decision-making process of the EC which has to be endured. The other side of the coin is accessibility, which can be a vital protection.

It is sometimes hard to bring the press stories and comments 'back to earth' and reality, and this can be a difficult, not to say damaging time for the Commission and its representatives who may have an insufficiently complete draft to be able to correct the facts and make useful comments in response to the hot air, BUT it may force the draft into the open. Those with valid points to make would be wise to regard press reports with scepticism and get hold of the actual paper or proposal, read it with care, and possibly wait for the next, calmer, stage.

Stage 3 is when the most important amendments to the Commission draft are likely. It will be being considered by the EP, and now is the time to consult your MEP. You can do this in three ways: by writing to the MEP in whose constituency you live, by writing to whoever serves on the appropriate EP Committee, or by writing to one of the political groups.

Your MEP's power will depend on the attitude of the parties in the EP, and the powers of the EP as a whole, which will depend on the subject under discussion and the procedures prescribed in the Treaties. However, it is important to remember that your MEP will also be influenced by the national MPs and will have close links with his national counterparts, and indeed national government departments, so your local MP may also be able to help.

At Westminster as soon as Commission proposals become public, they are deposited with Scrutiny Committees in both the House of Commons and the House of Lords for examination. The Lords' Committee in particular often produces a detailed report on proposed legislation. It takes evidence from experts, Ministers and civil servants, and maintains informal contacts with industrial and business groups. Lords' reports are read by those who count. Get your work in if you can.

Stage 4 is when COREPER has the task of getting the Commission proposals into final shape for presentation to the Council for decision. The UK Permanent Representative (UKREP) is 'our man' in COREPER. He and his staff coordinate the views of all relevant UK interests and give on-the-spot briefings to UK Ministers. The staff of UKREP are extensive, and have direct links with UK departments. Many of the experts who work in UKREP are seconded from MAFF, the Department of Trade and Industry and the Ministry for the Environment. They can get detailed and expert advice at short notice, and there is a shuttle service of civil servants between Brussels and London (not to mention Edinburgh, Cardiff and Belfast) all of whom touch down in UKREP at some point.

The UKREP staff are exceptionally busy but if you do have important things to say about proposed legislation, they will do their best to help and are ideally placed to direct you to the pressure points in the Commission or the appropriate UK department.

Remember that this may realistically be your last chance to put your case to the Commission. Commissioners in particular are expected to be expert in the political situation and the problems of the country they know best, and to be well informed on how the Ministers of that country are likely to play their hands at the negotiating table, so it is well worth ensuring that they have your well-written, preferably brief and obviously efficiently set out views. Procedures vary, so watch proposal's progress.

It is, however, wise for those who wish to lobby on behalf of their industry, business or local authority to discover the area of ground on which the Commission will stand firm, the areas on which it will move, and the areas which will be gracefully conceded as a bargaining counter. Here contacts in Brussels are, undeniably, of great value. There is no point in spending time and money undermining the wrong wall of the citadel – the one due to collapse at the first trumpet blast.

It should be remembered that in some areas, such as competition law, the changes will be legislated for by the Commission itself, within its competence under the Treaties, so it is important to keep a close watch on developments, and in this sort of specialized area, you will probably have to rely on your professional advisers. If mistakes are made, then it is possible in Community matters to take action in the ECJ, but as always, it is far easier to ensure mistakes are avoided than to rectify them later.

It is emphasized that if possible at the least guidance should be sought from an accredited lobbyist. It should be noted that there is a code of conduct for lobbyists which should be adhered to. If you are a business which might be affected by changing international standards, it is wise to keep in touch with your local national standards authority (the BSI in the UK) as they often have considerable difficulty in getting useful input until it is too late.

Finally, the legislative processes have undergone changes in the past, and with ratification of the Amsterdam Treaty will be further changed so as to give greater powers to the EP (to put right the perceived democratic deficit) and to streamline the procedures. See Figure 6.

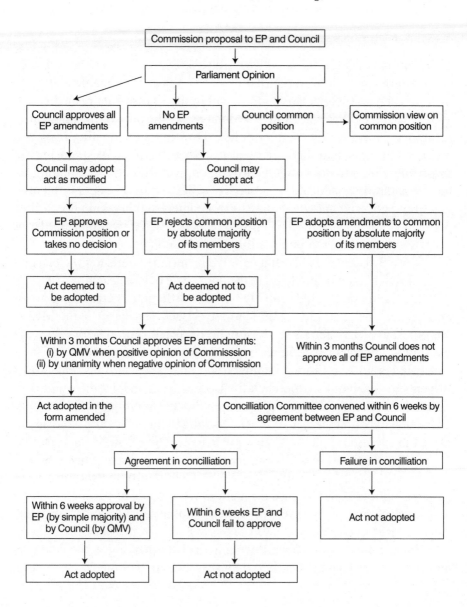

Figure 6 Revised co-decision procedure

SUMMARY

There are major differences between the shaping of national laws and of Community legislation. In the first case, the object is to enable a government to carry out its declared policy within the limits of its resources, no matter what the other parties involved may say. The duty of the opposition is almost always to oppose that policy. Drafting and enacting laws is a restricted process, and the individual back-bench MP at Westminster has surprisingly little to do with it. Consultation, fact-finding and opinion taking are naturally conducted on a massive scale, but may be less influential in a strong government which may be more interested in taking forward its political views. Cabinet policy, once agreed, is enacted by Simple Order or may be followed by the publication of a White Paper which will be followed by a Bill debated in Parliament. If a government fails to gets its legislation through, then it should go to the country ie hold an election.

In the EU matters could scarcely be more different. There is no government, no cabinet, and little confidentiality. 'Back-benchers' (ie the MEPs) not only have easy access to those who draft legislation while they are drafting it; they can exact, in writing, a promise that the problems of their constituents will be properly understood and taken into account. Constituents themselves can approach the Commission and get their points of view across, directly. Those who question aspects of proposed Community legislation may find their government backing them to the hilt, and ready to use all its clout through the Council machinery. Any firm, local authority, trade or professional association, trade union, quango, or what-you-will that feels it may be seriously affected by Community legislation has an absolute right to plead its case throughout the process of decision-making with the backing of experts and pressure groups at a local, national or international level.

In short, opportunities for influencing decision-making in the Community are not only guaranteed, they are an essential part of the process itself.

Part V

Individual policies

THE EU AND BUSINESS NEEDS

Introduction

The Community's range of activities is wide. Though they all derive from the Treaties, there is nothing immutable about them. Indeed, trying to adapt swiftly to changing circumstances in the EU itself and the world at large takes up an enormous amount of the energy and imagination of those working within the ambit of the EU – and indeed EEA.

What follows is a brief and doubtless subjective look at some current Community policies. Those requiring more detailed information on each policy might wish to refer to the *EC/EU Fact Book* by Alex Roney, also published by Kogan Page, or specialist books, and there is a list of publications at the end of this book, together with an indication of some of the databases available for consultation via the Internet.

Employment and Social Policy

The improvement of living and working conditions and equality of opportunity for the citizens of the Member States were an aim of the Rome Treaty. The whole concept of the Social Policy of the Community has developed since then, and now covers such matters as health and safety in the workplace (and indeed elsewhere), working conditions, protection for women and children, provisions relating to the disabled, to combat racism and other unfair discrimination, to coordinate the policies on social benefits and pensions, recognition of qualifications gained in other Member States, employee protection and consultation rights, collective bargaining, vocational training... the list goes on.

With a workforce of over 150 million people, and unemployment at around 17 million in the Member States (10.2 per cent of the labour force in the EU in April 1998, ranging from Spain with 18.9 per cent to Luxembourg with 2.3 per cent), one of the main priorities in the EU is to stimulate growth and employment in the European economy. This aim has been reiterated by the Council and there is a growing acceptance of the unpalatable fact that unemployment leads to other problems, such as urban decay, unsociable and criminal behaviour, an increase in drink and drug-related offences, and a spiral of social exclusion and other social ills which are increasingly expensive to remedy, and cause untold suffering.

Pensions are also a problem, as demographic change leads to higher social expenditure, at the same time as expectations are growing. The same applies to medical and other social costs. The stimulation of economic growth needed to help to pay for these increased costs, and to lower at least some of them by getting people back to work, is therefore supported by all Member States, and so by a number of Community initiatives. For example the Growth Initiative at the 1992 Edinburgh Summit led to the setting up of an investment fund to finance infrastructure projects in the Community and to provide loans to small and medium-sized enterprises (see page 59). Much has been done since, and various programmes have been set up to reduce unemployment, particularly when the Community policies themselves have been the cause of increased unemployment – for example when the need to reduce fish quotas have put fishermen out of work, or where the re-structuring of the coal and steel sectors to make them competitive in world markets have led to closures. A 1998 Action Plan aims to encourage entrepreneurs.

Outside factors can cause unemployment, for example where the textile industry has been under pressure from cheap imports (see page 62), and the various measures available such as anti-dumping procedures are not always effective or available to protect the industry concerned in the context of world trade, with the result that large-scale redundancies have to be made. The 1997 IGC came out very strongly in favour of the need to enhance and coordinate employment creating strategies in the Member States, and an Employment Agenda 2000 followed the dictat of the Amsterdam Resolution that the completion of the Single Market, monetary discipline and job creation have to be pursued in parallel, with joint and coordinated action by all involved in the drive towards creating jobs. Agenda 2000 is a strategy for strengthening growth, competitiveness and employment.

In April 1998 the Commission adopted the Social Action Programme 1998–2000, which sets out a strategic framework for European social policy, building on the aims of the Amsterdam Treaty and on European employment strategy. It has the three priority targets of promoting jobs, skills and mobility; assisting with the changing world of work; and developing an inclusive society. Quality of life and promoting a good standard of living are the keynotes of this programme, which particularly aims to encourage access to employment and employability.

The principle remains that economic growth must not be pursued to the detriment of social progress. The need to ensure that they go hand in hand was also set out in the Single European Act 1987, the aim of which was to accelerate the adoption of legislation to create the Single Market. In 1989 all the Member States except the UK signed a Community Charter on the Fundamental Social Rights of Workers (usually called the Social Charter), which tried to make some sense of the fragmented social policy which had been developing up until then. The Charter set out thirteen basic rights:

1. the right of every EC citizen to move freely throughout the Community, subject only to restrictions based on public policy, public safety or public security
2. the right to work in the EC country of one's choice, or to exercise any trade or occupation on the same terms as the nationals in the host state
3. the right to a fair wage
4. the right to improved living and working conditions
5. the right to the same social protection for EU citizens from other states and host state nationals in gainful employment
6. the right to freedom of association and collective bargaining, and to take collective action. This is linked to the establishment of industrial dispute settlement procedures
7. the right to vocational training
8. the right of men and women to equal treatment and opportunities
9. the development of the rights of workers to information, consultation and participation
10. the right to health protection and safety at work, and a movement towards minimum standards in all member states
11. provisions on protection for children and adolescents
12. the guarantee of minimum living standards for the elderly, and provision of a minimum income
13. improved social and professional integration for the disabled.

The Social Charter should be distinguished from the Social Chapter which was the protocol inserted in to the Union Treaty which was essentially a resolution signed by 14 of the 15 Member States (the UK then opting out) setting out the aims of social policy. These were:

1. to improve the competitiveness of the EU and to increase the chances of job-generating growth
2. to protect workers' rights through minimum social standards
3. to respect the principles of subsidiarity and proportionality
4. to aim for convergence of systems rather than making them uniform
5. gearing up the social dialogue and agreeing economic and social measures among themselves.

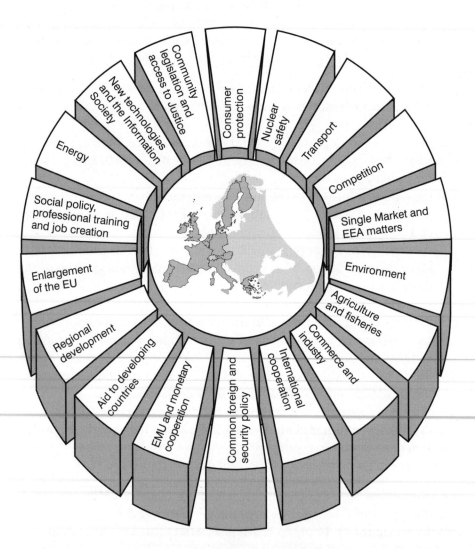

Figure 7 The main activities of the European Community

It was then agreed that while efforts would be made to achieve unanimity, if the UK could not agree, then the UK would drop out of negotiations, and the other 14 would go ahead by way of a special majority if necessary. Thus the Union Treaty extended majority voting of the 14 to matters such as the improvement of the working environment to protect workers' health and safety, improvement of working conditions, of information and consultation of employees and to measures to promote the integration of the people excluded from the labour market. The UK opt out situation has now changed with agreement to the Amsterdam Treaty which brings in this protocol to the treaty, and extends the Commission's competence in the field of social affairs to include action to prevent discrimination on the grounds of race, religion, sex or disability.

The creation of an Employment Committee provides a forum to assist with coordination and monitoring of employment policies in the EU, which must themselves respond to global challenges, and create an efficient, mobile, workforce. Work continues, as foreshadowed in the Green Paper 'Partnership for a New Organisation of Work' (1997) to look at new forms of work organization – such as teleworking, an increase in subcontracting, and outsourcing with the new employer–employee relationships created, and the possible need for new legislation to deal with these changes. The working week as well as health and safety impacts and management practice are being looked at with the Working Time Directive now effective.

It is interesting to note that the Social Partners (employers, employees, trade union and employer organizations and public enterprise representatives) can now put forward an agreement to the Council, which may then go forward to legislate to implement that agreement. The first directive to illustrate this procedure is the Parental Leave Directive 1996.

Equality and the importance of outlawing discrimination against people on the basis of their sex have long been a part of Community legislation, and there have been various provisions to ensure equal treatment for men and women. Various resolutions and declarations relating to race discrimination have also been adopted, and all Member States are signatories to the Council of Europe's Convention on the Protection of Human Rights and Fundamental Freedoms. When the Amsterdam Treaty comes into effect, the Council will be able to take action by unanimity to combat discrimination based on sex, racial or ethnic origin, religion or belief, disability, age or sexual orientation. A Commission action plan to combat racism in the EU is likely to have four specific aims: to include the relevance of combating racism in all the other EU policies and programmes; developing and exchanging information about the most effective anti-racist practices; and strengthening information and communication.

As to benefit systems: some Community provisions apply, but the Commission's third (1998) Report on Social Protection in Europe relating to 1997, reiterates the need to review and reform benefit systems to ensure they support the drive towards employment.

Another initiative which has not had much publicity but has provided some useful data has been the 1995 European strategy of encouraging local development and employment initiatives (LCEI).

Employee consultation and participation

It is first important to distinguish between employee participation – which relates to the participation of employees or their representatives in decision-making, and employee consultation – whereby the employees or their representatives are consulted, and may negotiate, but do not take the decisions.

The pros and cons of participation of employees in decision-making in enterprises, as distinct again from participation in the profits of the enterprise (through profit sharing or share distribution schemes, for example) have long been an area where widely differing views have been held in the different Member States. Indeed, over 20 years ago, in 1975 the Commission set out, in its Green Paper entitled 'Employee Participation and Company Structure' the reasons why it felt the Community should be involved in 'the undeniably controversial and difficult issue of the role of employees in relation to the decision-making structures of companies'. These were based on the need for harmonization of structures of companies and the moral right of those who would be affected by decisions to have some part in making them. This was referred to as the need for industrial democracy. The value of the workers in terms of input was also significant. In countries with a strong tradition of employer–employee consultation or even participation such as Germany, which already had two-tier boards providing for employee participation in decision-making, the proposals seemed a logical step forward. In other countries, such as the UK but also in Italy and Greece, the thought of employee participation in decision-making was anathema. The whole argument seems to have died down in recent years, and it is unlikely that employee participation proposals will be progressed quickly given the more recent emphasis on employee consultation instead. However, it may be interesting to note the main initiatives taken with regard to participation. The 5th Draft Directive on company law has been under discussion for many years, with drafts produced in 1972, 1983 and 1991. It included the principle of decision-making by employees in PLCs employing over 1000 staff in the EU either directly or through subsidiaries. It is not scheduled for agreement in the near future. Similar in concept to the 5th Directive in some ways was the Vredeling Draft Directive 1980 on procedures for informing and consulting employees, but this was disliked by various countries, and appears to have been shelved.

The European Company Statute, which is for a voluntary form of company, also includes provision for participation of employees in decision-making. It remains under discussion and could be agreed in the not too distant future. The first drafts were brought out in 1970, but it has changed considerably since then. The 1991 draft split the proposals into two, with a draft regulation for a European company statute, and a Draft Directive to complement it, with proposals relating to the involvement of employees. Besides its likely impact on employee participation provisions, which the UK has traditionally disliked, there remain credit-worthiness and liability concerns about the proposals in some Member States.

The view that is now increasingly accepted (particularly since the New Labour Government took over in the UK) is that employee consultation, at least, is a 'good thing', and reflects good management practice. Concentration now is on maintaining and creating jobs, while keeping enterprises competitive in a global context. Equally, employees have been more interested in getting and then keeping jobs, in which they are often overstretched anyway, rather than in taking on more responsibilities.

In the context of consultation, employees have considerable rights, some of which go back many years. The improvement of living and working conditions and equality of opportunities were objectives set out in the Treaty of Rome. The right of freedom of association and collective bargaining (in other words to belong – or not to belong – to the trade union of choice), and to have rights in collective bargaining and the institution of conciliation and arbitration procedures were set out clearly in the Social Charter agreed by 14 of the 15 Member States (the UK opting out, but this position changed with the Amsterdam Treaty) which was annexed as a protocol to the Union Treaty.

Besides these statements of policy, there were various directives enshrining the right of employees to be consulted. The Collective Redundancies Directive 1975 introduced minimum duties for employers to consult with representatives of the employees concerned where major redundancies were planned together with requirements to notify the relevant public authority, and provided for delays to facilitate negotiations, and possibly ameliorate consequences. The 1992 Directive on Collective Dismissals in Multinationals extended procedures and information requirements to employees working for the same employer in different Member States.

The EC Business Transfer (Acquired Rights of Employees in Transfers and Mergers) Directive 1977 meant that transferees generally automatically took over the existing contracts of staff employed. This Directive has been extended and more closely defined by a 1997 Directive, and the provisions became so complicated that the Commission has produced an explanatory memorandum. A further amendment to the Acquired Rights Directive agreed in June 1998 concerns outsourced and contract employees transferred from the public to the private sector, for example.

There are various other directives which protect the rights of employees. In terms of employee consultation the most significant is the European Works Council Directive 1994 which requires companies with other sites in at least two EU countries with 150 or more employees in the Member States, and at least 1000 staff overall, to set up works councils to enable consultation of employees. The Directive also sets minimum conditions for worker consultation and information. This directive may well be extended as it has been proposed that all companies in the EU with over 50 employees should be required to set up employee information and consultation committees.

Harmonization of company law

Harmonization of company law is a logical and progressive step where there is a single market as it is preferable to ensure that the expectations of the parties to contracts are met, particularly in terms of the business environment in which they are operating. The greater the harmonization and indeed assimilation of company law provisions, agency rules and general commercial provisions, including consumer protection, credit, and access to justice, the more confident will be the citizens of the EU, whether or not they are business people, in their dealings with each other. They will be less likely to get 'nasty shocks' over their rights or liabilities.

A series of directives since 1968 have provided for various safeguards and protection mechanisms and have harmonized disclosure provisions, classification of companies and capital requirements, the drawing up, auditing and publication of accounts (with exemptions for small companies), on consolidated accounts and the qualifications of auditors. Branch disclosure requirements for companies based in different Member States have been agreed. The ability to set up a private limited company with only one member (12th Directive 1989 on single member Companies) necessitated major changes to UK company law.

The European Company Statute noted above which seeks to provide a European form of limited companies remains under discussion, but a different European structure, the European Economic Interest Grouping (EEIG) adopted in 1985 as a regulation, came into force in 1989. Aimed at facilitating transnational cooperation between SMEs in particular in different Member States, it was based on an existing French structure. It has proved quite popular, despite the daunting fact that it can sometimes be governed by a number of different laws, and its members have unlimited joint and several liability for its debts. There are strict rules which govern its use, which is stipulated as being for the purpose of facilitating or developing the economic activities of its members, but on a non-profit-making basis. Thus it is a useful vehicle for cooperation in research projects for example.

The need to ensure that companies have secure management with controls relating to disclosure of shareholdings led to the Disclosure of Major Shareholdings Directive 1988 which introduced minimum rules for disclosure of changes in shareholdings of companies listed on a stock exchange. There are also discussions on the harmonizing of the role and liabilities of statutory auditors, and a move towards cohesion in auditing practices across the community. Assimilation of the rules of corporate governance remains under discussion.

International crime with big bucks – company fraud and money laundering – have become recognized problems where money can be moved swiftly from one jurisdiction to another. There are various controls on banks and financial institutions, and the Money Laundering Directive 1991 requires credit and financial institutions and banks to report suspicious transactions to the proper authorities, and to keep records for five years. There is an Administrative Cooperation Regulation 1992 which facilitates cooperation between fiscal authorities in the Member States, and police cooperation is increasing as the Europol Convention becomes ratified in more Member States. Although this is technically limited, mainly to terrorists, the European Drugs Unit has the remit to combat illegal trafficking in people, drugs and nuclear materials, and the sexual exploitation of children. The area of cooperation is being extended all the time in practice to keep up with increasingly mobile villains.

Industry, commerce and enterprise

Some manufacturing industries in the EU have been subjected to strong competitive pressure from other countries, particularly where labour and production costs have been less. Steel, shipbuilding and textile industries have all suffered in this way, with a consequential rise in unemployment in the areas affected. Unemployment is all too frequently followed by attendant social problems.

The thinking, therefore, behind the enterprise and industrial policy of the EU has been that to reduce social costs, you must increase employment, and to increase employment you must create a successful economic and social environment for business development. Various reviews, consultative documents and reports have looked with concern at the more effective enterprise cultures of the USA and Japan. They resulted in the First Action Plan for Innovation in Europe: Innovation for Growth and Development 1996. This aimed to improve the business culture in society and the economy, to improve regulatory, legal and fiscal provisions for innovation, and to promote more effective correspondence between research and innovation and business, ie exploitation of ideas and developments.

In 1997 the Business Environment Task Force (BEST) was set up to look at reducing the burdens on business, and much has been done through the Simpler Legislation for the Internal Market (SLIM) initiative. The 1997 Action plan for a Single Market aimed to remove any remaining barriers to the Single Market. The competitiveness of EU enterprises in a global market context, the development of international standards and improved taxation and financing incentives are seen as important areas, and work continues in many spheres, not least in the forum of the World Trade Organization to achieve and enforce international trading rules and to develop new markets world-wide.

Just a few of the initiatives will be explored below.

Commerce generally

Commerce is such a part of the whole working of the Single Market that it tends to be ignored as a separate subject. It is, in fact, the second largest economic sector in the EU. The Commission therefore produced a Green

Paper on Commerce in 1997 to consider this sector, its importance, structure and development, the challenges facing this sector and the actions
which should be taken by the EU, Member States or their public administration or even the enterprises themselves to enable them to meet the
challenges of the future. The Green Paper is comprehensive and makes
useful reading, as it considers, for example the position of various retail
sectors, independent organized commerce and franchise development.
Much of the support for commerce by the EU centres on assistance for
SMEs. The Committee on Commerce and Distribution (CCD) has been set
up which the Commission consults on all Community legislative or other
initiatives regarding commerce. This high-level committee has various
working groups and sub-groups and has the task of considering the best
ways of achieving the objectives set, and does impact assessments for proposed legislation.

There is also a European Federation (EuroCommerce) which represents
wholesaling and retailing, which is useful source of information. Euro-
Commerce and Eurofiet (the EU trade union organization representing
those employed in this area) have had productive dialogues since 1983
mostly concerning the training of staff in this area.

Small and Medium-Sized Industries (SMEs)

Because there were so many different definitions of SMEs, in 1996 a defin-
itive definition was agreed. Under this, Very Small Enterprises – also called
Micro-Enterprises – have under ten employees. Small Enterprises have
under 50 employees and an annual turnover of under ECU7m, or a balance
sheet total of under ECU5m. Medium-Sized Enterprises have from 51 to
250 employees and an annual turnover below ECU40m, or a balance sheet
total of up to ECU27m. The definition can be important, as it may be the
dividing line for access to grant assistance, for example.

The encouragement of SMEs is seen as a key factor in the strategy to
reduce unemployment and to revitalize Europe's economy, because so
many individuals – over 12 per cent of the EU workforce – work in their
own enterprise. Thus there is a renewed drive to reduce the burdens on business, seen to impact particularly harshly on SMEs, and to ensure, through
compliance cost assessments for example, that new proposals are cost
effective and do not unduly affect SMEs.

Many studies have been undertaken to establish what steps could be
taken to help SMEs and to identify their particular problems. Some obvious

difficulties were recurrent: obtaining inexpensive finance was the most common. The EC therefore promoted the provision of seed and venture capital funds, and the establishment of mutual guarantee companies. For example the EU contributed ECU1.27m from the Structural Funds to assist the New Enterprise Strategy (NES) on Teeside which has created 2823 jobs, and helped 1600 businesses to set up since April 1995. Perhaps surprisingly, in March 1998 around 75 per cent of those businesses were still operating.

EUROCONFIN assists the co-ordination of financial backing. The EIB can sometimes assist with financing of larger sums. A guidance on best practice has been produced and the European Association of Securities Dealers Automatic Quotation is effectively a new stock market for smaller companies wishing to obtain equity financing.

In April 1998 the Commission launched an action plan for discussion to encourage the development of a pan-European risk capital market, with six targets:

- integration of the risk capital market in Europe
- eliminating regular and institutional barriers
- achieving an improved taxation regime for risk capital
- promotion of high tech SMEs
- development of people with expertise and entrepreneurial flair
- reduction of cultural barriers to enterprise.

Other main problems of SMEs centre on inefficient management and bad marketing. Thus a small company could have an excellent product and still fail. Training has therefore been identified as a priority need, and the Commission has put together a network of training organizations in the EU to help SMEs which may be able to get training grants through the Structural Funds and the European Social Fund. Lifetime training is seen as a 'must' to ensure that there continues to be a mobile, up-to-date workforce in the EU which is able to make full use of swiftly developing technology.

The 1997–2000 Programme in favour of SMEs and the Craft Sector brings together existing initiatives to coordinate EU and national action. It includes action to reinforce priority areas, including help for commerce as one in three SMEs is involved in this sector. It is interesting to note the impact of the increasing power of consumers and consumer demands and concerns in the area. The Green Paper on Commerce (Com 96) published in the EU Supplement 2/97 gives a useful overview.

Language training

Language training is seen as another priority in the multi-lingual 'home' market of the EU with 11 main languages and 32 minority languages at this time, with more to come as the EU expands eastwards. Thus the SOCRATES–LINGUA Programme encourages language training mainly in the education sector, for students and teachers as part of the Socrates mobility programme which is effective throughout the EEA. About 127 000 students and 10 000 teachers participate in mobility programmes, so the next generation of employees will be better equipped linguistically.

Europartenariat

Another useful initiative is the scheme known as Europartenariat, designed to stimulate business cooperation and create partnerships among SMEs, particularly those in less favoured regions. Thus any group of SMEs from such a region, or a region in industrial decline may request a Europartenariat, and the appropriate SMEs are then chosen to participate with encouragement to those elsewhere to come to what is effectively a wide-ranging trade fair supported by EC funds.

The Financial Perspective for 2000–2006 for the EU retains support for these policies to assist SMEs, and emphasizes the importance of the impetus towards growth and employment.

The Commission has a telephone helpline for SMEs (01032 22 36 5151).

EXAMPLES OF DIFFERENT SECTORS

The steel industry

In this individual large industry, between 1974 and 1983, the numbers of steel workers in the EC fell from 800 000 to 480 000, and has fallen further since. The planned restructuring of the industry has not been totally successful. Restructuring grants and controls on state aid continue, as does the RESIDER programme specifically designed to assist regions with reduced iron and steel production. It should be noted that following the lapse of the

European Coal and Steel Community Treaty in 2002, the Commission will take over its competences within the ambit of the European Communities, but as a separate sector.

Textile and clothing industry

Here again restructuring has been necessary, with the RETEX programme (extended to 1999) specifically geared to promoting diversification of activities in regions which are over-dependent on the textile and clothing industry. Thus it helps with training, rehabilitation of abandoned industrial premises, improvement of polluting processes and encourages viable enterprises in these regions to adapt to other business sectors. The use of anti-dumping measures to control cheap imports from third countries, though available, are not often used, as there is concern that the Single Market should not be charged with being 'Fortress Europe'.

Shipping

The competition from Japan and Korea has been intense, and EC funds have been concentrated on giving conversion assistance to areas affected, and providing social measures for workers made redundant from the industry.

Regarding the quality of shipping in the EU: this aims at being much higher than the level of safety required under internationally agreed standards, both in terms of general safety, environmental protection and living and working conditions for employees. In seeking to ensure these standards are maintained, the EU has been promoting 'Port State Control', ie inspections in ports. Much is also being done in terms of research to promote good quality shipping – thus the approximate allocations in ECU for this work for 1994–99 were: 18m for logistic concepts and systems; 11m for safety and protection of the environment; 11m for traffic management and information systems; and 11m for human resources. The aim is to improve maritime training, reduce casualties and promote formal safety environmental assessments. Various directives and conventions exist to help to prevent accidents with regard to dangerous and polluting goods or substances carried by sea, with regard to notification, and discharge for example. Traffic flow is another aspect, and satellite and terrestrial navigation systems are seen as essential. Increasingly, vessels can be monitored both to ensure their safety, and the safety of others.

Tourism

Some 200 million EU citizens go on holiday each year, so one of the industries gaining in importance in the EU is the tourist industry, which provides a conservative estimate of 9 million jobs in the EU. It was agreed for the first time in 1992 that there should be a Community policy to support tourism and the Regional Funds have supported measures to reduce the seasonal nature of tourism, and to exploit the natural cultural historic and architectural heritage to encourage tourism both in and outside of urban areas, particularly 'green' tourism. Now the PHILOXENIA Programme 1997–2000 helps in this area. It includes the promotion of Europe as a tourist destination for travellers from other countries among its four objectives. It also supports the implementation of environmentally friendly management systems for tourist accommodation.

Transport

The importance of good transport links has always been recognized, and Article 3 of the Treaty of Rome required Member States to adopt a 'Common Policy' in the sphere of transport. It has perhaps, proved to be a surprisingly difficult area, as it encompasses not only infrastructure for road, rail, inland waterways and maritime ports and air transport, but also, with the internal market, the need to achieve liberalization.

It is interesting to note that in 1985 the Council of Ministers was found guilty by the Court of Justice for failing in its duty to create a common transport policy. However, since then much has been done. The 1992 Union Treaty emphasized the importance of having a safe effective transport infrastructure, the development of which must take into account environmental considerations.

The Commission's Communication in 1992 on the future development of the Common Transport Policy (Com 92 494 Final 2 December 1992) was followed by an action plan in 1994 with seven aims:

1. to guarantee correct implementation of the Single Market rules to ensure that measures introduced are enforced to create the free movement of passengers and goods
2. to develop genuine integrated transport systems for the Community as a whole with particular emphasis on combining several modes of transport
3. to strengthen the transport infrastructure, by improving links between peripheral and central regions of the Community, developing Trans-European Networks (TENs) to interconnect national networks

4. to introduce transport systems which respect the environment
5   to improve the safety and security of all means of transport
6. to adopt measures in the social field to ensure better working conditions and training, and increase protection of transport workers
7. to develop the external dimension of the Common Transport Policy in relations with third countries by eliminating bilateral agreements and working towards central negotiation of all agreements.

This last aim was flouted for some time with bilateral air transport agreements being negotiated with the USA, for example. However, in 1994 master plans for TENs were adopted covering land, sea and air, and these are now being extended to Central and Eastern European countries. Transport TENs should be distinguished from the TENs which relate to energy, information and telecommunications. The master plans covered:

- rail – conventional, high speed and combined
- highways
- inland waterways and seaports
- airport infrastructures.

The aims behind the transport networks are:

- to achieve cheaper, faster and safer transport
- to strengthen links with peripheral or sparsely populated regions
- to keep environmental protection considerations in mind
- to establish links with both Central and Eastern European and Mediterranean States.

Financing has proved a problem as it is estimated that about ECU400 billion will be needed to complete the TENs for transport by 2010, and private–public partnerships are being encouraged.

While there is progress in achieving a single market in transport – indeed, it should have been achieved – the three aims of the Community Transport Action Programme 1995–2000 reflect continuing problems. These aims are:

- to improve the quality of transport systems as regards competitiveness, safety and environmental impact
- to improve the functioning of the Single Market in transport
- to broaden the external dimension by improving links with third countries.

The current impetus is towards environmentally friendly forms of transport; the encouragement of the use of public as opposed to private transport in urban areas; and the encouragement of research into and use of biofuels – it being recognized that transport constitutes a significant source of harmful pollution in the EU. However, it should be noted that the interests of transport workers are not being forgotten, for example a draft Directive to prevent unfair competition in ferry services in the EU was proposed in April 1998 which would ensure that crew members from outside the EU are employed on the same conditions as those from the Member State of registration of the vessel. This is to prevent exploitation of foreign staff, and the escalation of employment of foreign staff to keep down employment costs, with consequent job losses for nationals.

SCIENCE AND TECHNOLOGY

Science and technology and the Framework Programmes

In 1973 the UK joined the EC and Messrs Heath, Brandt and Pompidou (Prime Ministers) signed a joint statement warning that unless the countries of the Community quickly formed a team they would lose sight of their competitors in the new technologies (notably the USA with a commanding lead, but being remorselessly tracked by Japan), but nothing much happened for over a decade. Since then there have been several programmes.

As early as 1974 at the request of Council, the Commission produced two draft programmes. The first was to mobilize skills, research and technology at the Community level. The second was for the joint development of 'informatics' – the omnibus word covering such things as the electronic processing of information, office automation, and telecommunications. These programmes called for collaborative research, feasibility studies, and coordination of procurement policies. These were regularly dusted off, considered in the Council with much thoughtful nodding of heads and dumped once again in the pending tray. National and company rivalries reduced collaboration to a polite formality.

The turn of the tide probably came in 1979 with the creation of Round Table discussions for the heads of electronic industries in the Community. The fact that tycoons were at least willing to talk to each other frankly and in confidence was the first sign of a changing mood and a changing market. Informatics in terms of world trade was already worth over $200 billion a year, and was growing at between 8 per cent and 10 per cent per annum.

The Community's share of high technology exports as a percentage of total exports had remained static at just under 25 per cent since 1963. The US share had risen from 29 per cent to 34 per cent, and Japan's share had risen from 16 per cent to 35 per cent. And the tempo was accelerating. This helped enormously, if a little late, to concentrate the minds of those round the table. Eight out of ten personal computers sold in Europe were being made in Japan. In the new industries as a whole, a positive balance of payments for the Community *vis à vis* the world as a whole had been turned into a $10 billion deficit.

Thus, in the early 1980s came the establishment of the first real Community strategy for the modern industries and the first hard results. The European Space agency and the Airbus industries began to get into their stride. As Information Access Network (EURONET-DIANE) was set up, and the impetus continued.

After the Single European Act 1987 and the launch of the programme for the completion of the internal market, Community research and technology policy took on a new dimension. A dynamic research policy is regarded as an investment in the future. Computers, telecommunications, industrial technologies, and biotechnology are key factors for improving the Community's industrial competitiveness. Furthermore, as the then Commission President Jacques Delors announced in 1991:'Science conducted on a co-operative basis could be the driving force for the construction of a real European culture since it achieves exactly the right combination of universality and specificity.'

In 1992 the Treaty on European Union in Article 130F established the Framework Programme with general objectives for research in the EU with the aims of:

1. strengthening the scientific and technological bases of industry in the EU
2. encouraging industry to become more competitive internationally and
3. supporting other Community policies.

It should be noted that while the activities supported by the programmes are all subject to the general principle of subsidiarity and are not intended to take the place of national research programmes, they are set against a formidable international background. Thus, in 1995 European research investment was 1.9 per cent of GDP, when it was 2.45 per cent in the USA and 2.95 per cent in Japan. In Japan in particular this proportion has increased significantly year after year. In 1996 Europe had 4.7 scientists per 1000 inhabitants, as against 7.4 in the USA and 8 in Japan. The competition in science and technology in China, India, Korea and Taiwan is growing. This scenario has led to the perceived need in the EU that not only must science and technology research and development be encouraged in the EU, but that to be effective, this support must be cohesively given, as the competition is significant and global. Developments must take into account economic and social objectives. The Information Society is burgeoning, and so is the need to have sustainable development. In fact the advent of the information society has meant vastly expanded communications with instant access to information world-wide. The world, in terms of data access, is often just an Internet call away.

The Fourth Framework Programme for Research, Technological Development and Demonstration (FPIV) 1994–1998; and immediately following on: the Fifth Framework Programme (FPV) on Research, Technological Development and Energy (1999–2003)

In discussions on the FPIV it was noted that 'the level of research is a sure guide to the confidence of a country or region in its own future' (*Inventing Tomorrow*, 1996 Commission General Information Booklet). Times move on, and it has since been noted that one out of every three new jobs created in the USA in the four years up until 1997 were in the high technology SMEs. So Research and Development (R&D) in this area has become a focus for job creation as well as economic competitiveness for the EU. It is important to know that only a short time ago, the EU was nearly US$25 billion in deficit in terms of its trade balance with the USA and Japan in high technology goods. However, the Framework Programmes (FPs) are not limited only to EU Member States – they are now open to most Central and Eastern European countries, for example where there are Europe agreements in place, to EEA countries, and now increasingly to subscribing third countries such as Switzerland and Israel. EU developments have to be considered, too, in the light of WTO agreements.

FPIV and FPV are important programmes and are supported by the determination of the Member States and their political will to work more closely together to ensure that there is both viable competition in the EU and a useful increase of jobs in this sector, with increased input and opportunities for SMEs. Great emphasis is placed on exploitation of the results of research.

FPIV and FPV are different in concept, as FPV, not finally agreed at the time of writing, is to be more objectives specific rather than project-based, but it is useful to consider PFIV first, albeit applications are virtually all closed.

The funding under FPIV was in the region of ECU13.1 billion (£10.9 billion) and it was aimed at enhancing the quality of life for European citizens by creating links between industry and academia, encouraging cooperation in developing and using new ideas. Funding is by one of six methods:

- shared cost (FPIV providing up to 50 per cent of costs)
- concerted actions: funding is put towards coordinating the project and not the project itself
- direct actions: EU pays for whole cost at one of its own sites
- specific measures: EU pays for specific researchers on particular projects
- accompanying, preparatory and support measures
- allowable costs – in some circumstances.

FPIV supports four areas or 'activities':

1. research and demonstration programmes including information and communication technologies, industrial technologies, environment, energy, transport and socio-economic research, life sciences and technologies. In this first activity there are 15 programmes, each with various strands
2. international scientific cooperation
3. dissemination and utilization of results
4. training and mobility.

There have been considerable successes in various areas, including the development, for example of telematics with its emphasis on development of user-friendly multimedia technology and the promotion of employment.

FPV is to be much more purpose-based – targeted on the need to underpin other Community policies. Two major themes are the Information Society, and the need to achieve sustainable development. It is recognized that innovative research costs have spiralled, and there is an increasing demand globally for biotechnological products. Thus it will have a budget of at least ECU14 billion, and be focused on:

1. resources of the living world and the need to achieve acceptable energy systems
2. competitive and sustainable growth
3. the Information Society and the need to make IT user friendly
5. development of individual human potential, and supporting the training and mobility of scientists
6. innovation
7. the participation of SMEs, particularly in the light of the employment drive.

Thus, for example, biotechnology, instead of being a separate area, will become part of many targeted areas, such as the cell factory, agricultural and fisheries developments, the environment and medical and health needs. The quality of life of EU citizens is a priority, as is the development of a user-friendly Information Society. The main key is likely to remain the promotion of greater scientific and technological cooperation in multi-sectoral and multi-disciplinary technologies of wide application. The importance of a clean and congenial workplace which stimulates innovation and extra employment is also stressed. The links between research and exploitation will be strengthened, and further improvements made to intellectual property rights (patents, trade marks, copyright and designs protection) to encourage inventors and research.

Problems remain, and work continues. For example it is intended to streamline administration and increase the flexibility of the programmes to enable swift support to be given to research when needed as a matter of urgency, for example when a particular problem arises such as BSE.

Some examples are given below of programmes running under FPlV.

Esprit: Information Technologies (IT) 1994

This has four priority areas for funding:

1. software technologies which provide proper, reliable user-friendly software
2. components and sub-systems technologies where the research is into components such as integrated microsystems and flat screens, and is aimed at building a competitive European industry
3. multimedia systems which are aimed at creating, storing and manipulating multimedial information and
4. long-term research.

Esprit information packs are available from the ISI Business Infoline on 0345 215 2000.

Brite-Euram: Industrial and Materials Technologies

This programme was launched in 1985. Its aim was to provide help for advanced technology in traditional industries – aeronautics, motor vehicles, chemicals, textiles engineering and the rest – and so provide an incentive to create a significant and advanced technological base to assist Community industry to maintain international competitiveness. The funds were aimed at pre-competitive research and development involving co-operation between participants in two or more Member States, in the hope that important technological breakthroughs would result.

Some successful projects have included automatic sewing systems for the textile industry, reliability testing methods for marine and off-shore structures, reducing friction in internal combustion engines, and developing compounds for the aeronautics industry at high temperatures.

The current programme has three priority research areas:

1. production technologies to help future industries, relating for example to the incorporation of new technologies into existing production systems, the development of 'clean' production technologies such as re-cycling product by-products for example, and the rational management of raw materials
2. technologies to promote product innovation, such as research into new technologies relating to the design and engineering of products and materials
3. technologies to improve transport through better aeronautics and designs for vehicles with better production and safety and environmental standards.

Biotechnology

Since the first programme in 1985, many hundreds of projects have been submitted, and many selected. Of these some are particularly noteworthy: the study of protein architecture, the application of biotechnology to industrial micro-organisms the risk associated with genetic manipulation. There are various programmes in this area of FPIV including BIOTECH which required applications to involve participation in at least two Member

States. Biomedicine and Health (BIOMED) which includes biomedical engineering and research into diseases, and FAIR for agriculture and fisheries production, and the utilization of biological raw material in the EU are examples. However, it should be noted again that biotechnology is now seen as so germane to so much research that it will be supported more in terms of being a tool to underpin other projects.

Information packs can be obtained from DGXII, and information on Biotechnology projects funding is available from:

Tim Willis,
Biotechnology and Biological Sciences Research Council,
Polaris House,
North Star Avenue,
Swindon SN2 1UH
Tel: 01793 413 284 Fax: 01793 413 382

or:

MAFF,
Science Division,
Nobel House,
17 Smith Square,
London SW1P3JR
Tel: 0171 238 5524 Fax: 0171 238 6129

General information is available from:
IMT Helpline,
National Physical Laboratory,
Queens Road,
Teddington TW11 OLW
Tel: 0181 943 6660 Fax: 0181 943 2989

Further details of funding strands are given in the European Information Booklet *Funding from the European Union* published by the Representation of the European Commission in the UK in collaboration with NatWest. As usual, information published by the Commission is also available on the Internet through Europaserver (http://europa.eu.int).

Telecommunications and Information Technology

The acronym IT is now on everyone's lips. Are you up to date? Can you use the Internet? Do you use the appopriate database? Telex is out, fax is a bit old-fashioned and E-mail is a must. So much has changed in the last ten years. Telecommunications are vital links, and the Trans-European Networks for information mean that speed of change as to the developments in technology available for use by every citizen is difficult to comprehend. The Commission has set up the Information Society Forum and the High Level Group of Experts to report on the impact of new technologies, for example on work patterns, and to advise on necessary Community action.

Liberalization in the telecommunications sector continues to have an impact on the cost and number of services. Mobile telephone users alone are likely to number at least 40 million by 2000. The European Committee for Telecommunications Regulatory Affairs (ECTRA) is already harmonizing national licensing conditions for networks. Global telecommunications are the subject of a WTO agreement signed by over 68 countries, whereby the EU, US and Japanese markets will be open to foreign competition.

Satellite communications

Very important to the development of telecommunications and swift transmission of data and media presentations, satellite communication is the subject of a 1997 Action plan to promote the EU as a global participant, and various provisions deal with regulation.

Television and audio-visual policy

Television and audio-visual policy is seen as very important, as around 350 million people in the EU watch an average of two hours of TV every day. Thus the EU is looking to this sector to provide about around two million new jobs by 2000, and the Media II Programme for 1996–2000 concentrates on three areas – the training of audio-visual professionals, project development, and distribution, broadcasting and post-production activities.

High Definition (HD) TV is regarded as the key to the improving standards increasingly required by the consumer, and the wide screen 16.9 format is taking over from the 4.3 screen. There are now 40 European television stations transmitting in 16.9, and the Community has supported around 20 000 hours of programmes. The widescreen Television 16.9 Action Plan is seen both as a boost to the European electronics and professional equipment industry, and for the audio-visual sector, and is run by the Commission DG10 – Audiovisual Policy.

The value of the television industry should not be underestimated – it is huge. Besides the electronics and media industries, it supports writers and performers, and advertising. This many-billion-pound industry is vital to commerce. Provisions do therefore exist to protect consumers and others in a number of ways. The 1997 Television without Frontiers Directive, revising a 1989 directive, set out a new legal framework for TV broadcasting in the EU.

Eureka

The EU does work with other countries in a number of initiatives. For example, this French initiative, launched in 1985 was first greeted somewhat coolly in the UK – partly, no doubt, because it was mistakenly portrayed in the press as 'France's answer to Star Wars'. Now the situation is very different. It is a framework for advanced cross-border collaborative research and technology in all sectors of industry, and complements the EU's R&D programmes. It involves 25 countries, namely: the 15 EU members, plus the Czech Republic, Hungary, Iceland, Norway, Poland, Romania, the Russian Federation, Slovenia, Switzerland, and Turkey.

Further information can be obtained from:
The UK EUREKA Unit,
3rd Floor,
Buckingham Palace Road,
London SW1W 9SS
Tel: 0171 215 1618 Fax 0171 215 1700

THE WORLD ABOUT US

Agricultural policy

The Common Agricultural Policy (CAP) was set up by the Rome Treaty in 1957 with the various aims of:

- improving productivity and technical progress
- optimizing labour use
- protecting the standard of living of farmers
- stabilizing agricultural markets so as to ensure free movement of agricultural goods
- preventing significant price fluctuations at the same time as ensuring continuity of supply at reasonable prices for the consumer.

All this was very laudable, and CAP was one of the first areas where Member States transferred some of their sovereignty to the European Community. However, in operation the CAP swallows up a large proportion of community funds, and has therefore been the target of vitriolic, usually well-earned, criticism ever since, possibly partly because of its early success. Thus over the past 25 years, European agriculture has undergone profound changes. The living standards of the farming community have improved, and the consumer has been able to rely on steady supplies of agricultural products at reasonable prices (although some would argue with this).

Over the years various reforms have been attempted with varying success. Beef mountains, wine lakes and over-production of milk and other commodities led to the introduction of quotas. Set aside, reductions in subsidies support and intervention prices, particularly of beef cereals and milk continue to be made. Fraud has been a major problem in the area, and the most recent proposals suggest that the rules are to be radically simplified, and applied in a more decentralized way, with Member States and regions being given an increased responsibility for implementation. The whole saga of BSE has caused strong feelings, with those advocating protection of the consumer, versus those arguing for free movement of goods, and insisting that the restrictions are caused by a desire to break the UK's lucrative beef export market.

There is considerable disquiet at this time as to the likely impact of the enlargement of the EU in terms of the cost of CAP, as it will lead to an estimated 50 per cent increase in the agricultural land area of the EU and a 100 per cent increase in the farm labour force. Thus in June 1998 the European Council set a nine-month deadline for reform of the CAP in line with the Agenda 2000 internal reform package which is considered necessary in the context of enlargement.

In the Commission Communication Agenda 2000 presented in July 1997, the CAP's future policy objectives were listed as:

- to improve the Union's competitiveness through lower prices
- to guarantee safety and quality of food to consumers
- to ensure stable incomes and a fair standard of living for the agricultural community
- to make production methods environmentally friendly and to respect animal welfare
- to integrate environmental goals into its instruments

• to seek to create alternative income and employment opportunities for farmers and their families.

It should perhaps be noted that protection of and access to agricultural markets have periodically caused problems in terms of international relations. For example bananas, rice, butter, lamb and even vintage wine have all caused difficulties in negotiations with third countries, all of whom want access to the large consumer market of the EU, and frequently object to the support given to EU farmers.

Agriculture has undergone enormous changes in the last few years, with recent recognition of the adverse effects of intensive farming, and the move towards more environmentally friendly farming methods. This is because agriculture is one of the main pollutant industries, largely due to the widespread use of pesticides, and chemical fertilizers, and intensive farming methods which cause enormous nitrate and waste problems, largely to water supplies, but also to land and air. This has led to a rise in illness among agricultural workers and possibly others, soil and animal fertility problems and increased levels of sickness in stock. Consumer concerns have led to less intensive, more 'natural' methods, sometimes scientifically applied, with, for example ecologically balanced greenhouses free of pesticides, using instead artificially introduced correct levels of appropriate insects to control pests. There are funding opportunities for those adopting agri-environmental programmes, and in some countries taxes have been introduced to reduce the levels of pesticides (Denmark); fertilizer (Sweden); and manure production (The Netherlands).

However, as farms grow in size and efficiency, so employment in the sector reduces. This has led to an increase in rural development aid to support the rural economies, and the EU supports such schemes in over 40 regions in the EU.

Fisheries policy

Fishing commands loyalties of a fiercer and deeper kind than any other industry. Although there are relatively few fishermen in the EU, the industry is crucial to many areas where entire communities depend upon it. The first common fisheries policy (CFP) was established in 1970, though very soon after negotiations over the UK, Danish, Norwegian and Irish membership of the EC were begun.

It was not until 1983 that a revised fisheries policy was introduced, and there have been various revisions since then. The objective of the CFP was to regulate catches, trade in fish products, and access to waters within the sovereignty of Member States. It now tries to achieve the sensible management and conservation of fish stocks. The current CFP arrangements provide measures to limit fishing activity and rules on the utilization of resources, as well as the surveillance of fishing activity.

Thus the CFP lays down the Total Allowable Catches (known as TACs) for Member States, and these are agreed annually by the Council of Ministers. Zones are established around the coasts to protect the interests of inshore fishermen, for example round the Shetland Islands. There is help for marketing organizations when prices fall, and funds for the improvement of boats, harbours, the food processing industry, and fishermen who wish to leave the industry.

Each Member State must declare its catches, and in addition to national monitoring, the Commission now employs a team of inspectors from Community countries who are independent of their own governments and form transnational inspection teams. A common marketing organization, administered by the producing organizations themselves, is responsible for guaranteeing fishermen a living when prices collapse.

During the first few years after the 1983 agreement was signed, the share out of fish stocks was agreed on time and in relative harmony. However, when Spain and Portugal joined the EC in 1986 they brought with them a fishing fleet larger than that of the other ten Member States, and increased the catch by nearly 30 per cent. Not surprisingly, the argument over the implications for the EC's fisheries sector of Spanish membership were protracted, and have caused enormous problems, many of which continue, despite efforts to control them, with problems of access in Community waters. Fish stocks have diminished alarmingly, despite more support for farmed fish projects.

During 1986 two important agreements were reached. The first was a package of technical measures to conserve fish stocks in Community waters, largely by increasing the mesh size of nets. The second approved a ten-year structural policy for the fisheries sector.

Various reports and action programmes have followed, but the situation remains unsatisfactory as regulations are often flouted. The installation of satellite surveillance systems may help in this area. The European Fisheries sector remains in an extremely vulnerable position both economically and socially especially in terms of employment. The social situation is particularly worrying since structural change in the sector often affects regions where alternative employment opportunities are limited.

The Fourth Multi-annual Guidance Programme (MAGIV) 1997–2002, taking heed of a Commission Report which highlighted problems and indicated guidelines, includes enormous catch reductions reflecting concern over the continuing depletion of fish stocks, and seeks to restore some balance between fish resources and fishing effort, attempting to cut back excess capacity, and taking greater control and enforcement of compliance with the rules.

It should be noted that the catch of EU fishermen in third country waters accounts for 25 per cent of the EU fish products, so international agreements remain very important to fisheries production. A maritime agricultural research programme has been successful, and the production of farmed fish is being encouraged. Equally, there is support for fishermen leaving the sea, and fleet reduction subsidies are available which are seen to be assisting in some measure.

In June 1998 a ban on drift net fishing on the high seas (with exceptions in the Baltic) has been agreed to protect dolphins, with a three and a half year implementation period. There will be aid for the fishermen affected in the UK, Ireland, France and Italy (the only countries still to operate drift nets).

The environment and environmental protection

Environmental protection is a nascent and important (and politically correct) industry which is growing in the EU. The principles of environmental policy were first defined in 1972 following a conference of Heads of State which affirmed the need to implement a common policy on the environment, but it was not until the Single European Act 1986 that the environmental dimension was formally introduced into EC policy. By early 1990 almost 130 items of Community legislation in the area of the environment had been enacted, and now there are around 340 provisions, including regulations, directives and decisions, in force. They range from measures to control the discharge of dangerous substances into air and water, to waste control, to the protection of wild birds.

As with many policies of the EU, there is a pattern to be seen, as the scale and effects of environmental damage became more important, not only in fact, but also politically, as politicians reacted to the grassroots pressure for change, culminating in the (now widely accepted) principle of 'the polluter must pay' through to the need for sustainability.

In 1993 the Chairman of the EP's environmental Committee was quoted as saying, 'In the 1980s, arguments about the cost of not integrating Europe led to the Internal Market. The argument for the 1990s has to be the cost of not integrating environmental policy.'

Thus the objectives of EU environmental policy are:

- to preserve, protect and improve the quality of the environment
- to contribute to protecting human health
- to ensure a prudent and rational utilization of natural resources.

To achieve these aims:

- pollution should be prevented at source
- environmental policy must be compatible with economic and social development
- all planning processes must take environmental considerations into account and
- the polluter must pay.

In 1985 the Environmental Impact Assessment Directive was passed, which requires that before work is begun on any major project an environmental impact assessment must be carried out to assess effects on:

- human beings, fauna and flora
- soil, water, air, climatic factors and the landscape
- the inter-relationship between these factors
- material assets and cultural heritage.

This directive applies to a wide variety of projects, and has had an impact, not least because of the requirements to inform the public of proposals, and the consequent public outcries and demonstrations which have caused rather more care to be taken at the planning stage.

The TEU strengthened the Community stance on the Environment, making it a specific requirement that environmental considerations be taken into account when formulating new policies or provisions. The Amsterdam Treaty further strengthened cooperation between Member States in the field of the environment, and sustainable development, and the European Council has urged further action to achieve sustainable development in accordance with the Earth Summit agreements.

The European Environment Agency, which is situated in Copenhagen, does useful work and promotes data exchange of relevant information in the EU and EEA, and works closely with other international bodies. It is now recognized that the need to protect the environment and to reduce global warming can no longer be looked at from a national perspective – it is a global problem, which needs a disciplined and world-wide approach, albeit national actions can help.

Thus new provisions are being made all the time. The different Member States are undertaking their own initiatives to assist in the reduction of pollution, whether it be of air, water or land. For example, in the UK the Land Fill Tax is one which seeks to encourage a reduction in waste – but there are many other increasingly coordinated carrots and sticks in the Member States. An area of concern, however, is the pollution risk in the aspirant countries in Central and Eastern Europe, and the costs of improving the situation in those countries.

The Fifth Environmental Action Plan 1992–2000 'Towards Sustainability' looks at medium- and long-term objectives in five areas: industry, agriculture, energy, transport and tourism. It specifically aims to strengthen the EU's role in international initiatives. In terms of national areas of concern, much is being done to reduce pollution. Agriculture is seen as one of the main polluting industries. Transport and energy production are others. Research into better farming methods and the CAP-reforming Agri-environmental programme supporting less intensive farming, cleaner industries, the use of bio-fuels in transport and cleaner energy production are all likely to help in the future. As the greatest impetus for environmental protection comes from publicity, and the environmental lobby, so the 1990 Directive on the Freedom of Access to Information on the Environment whereby anyone can gain access to information relating to the environment from public authorities or related bodies has been a useful step. Arguably an even more useful step will be provided by the regulatory framework for environmental audits which companies in the EU will be required to carry out, as it is hoped that this will prevent and even avoid pollution.

In 'Taking European Environment Policy into the 21st Century – A Summary of the Commission's Progress Report and Action Plan on the Fifth Programme of Policy and Action in Relation to the Environment and Sustainable Development' (Action Plan (COM (95) final) adopted by the Commission on 24th January 1996, environmental policy was stated to have 'the long time goal of transforming the European Economy into one whose development would be sustainable for generations to come'. A difficult goal which must somehow be achieved.

The urban environment tends to be forgotten, but work has been continuing in this sector, as urban regeneration is seen as important in the battle to increase employment and reduce exclusion. Thus new measures are being agreed to facilitate cross-border coordination of planning policies to revive cities and towns, with a common approach to transport, housing policies, water use, and so on, following from a first draft of a Commission document on the European Spatial Development Perspective.

Energy

The Community is constantly shaping its energy policy in response to the complex changes that are having a radical impact on the energy sector, from the development of the Internal Market to the historic changes in Eastern Europe and the former Soviet Union; to the increasing concern about global climatic change.

In 1992 the Commission published a special issue of *Energy in Europe* entitled 'A View to the Future' which presented a detailed analysis of the prospects for energy supply and demand trends to the year 2005.

The EU's energy policy was, and remains, based on three principles:

1. the development of the internal market in energy
2. the development of an external relations policy for energy
3. minimizing the negative impact on the environment of energy use and production.

Great progress has been made in the development of the internal market in energy, and market liberalization provisions have been achieved in electricity and gas supplies, in public procurement, and in the energy equipment sector. For example the 1996 Directive liberalizes the electricity market in stages, and there is a similar provision for gas, which is some years from full liberalization in the EU. There has been standardization of energy equipment and products, and agreement in various areas as to the principle of reduction of greenhouse gases.

The Commission in 1992 put forward a proposal for a carbon/energy tax, together with fiscal incentives for investments in energy-saving or carbon dioxide-reducing measures so as to shift demand away from the most polluting fuels. Since that time fiscal incentives have assumed greater importance, with incentives for the use of bio-fuels being encouraged. The latest initiatives concern the reduction of sulphur and other emissions to help those with asthma (which may increase some heating and transport costs) to bring the provisions into line with World Health Organization guidelines.

The 1995 Green Paper on the Future of Energy Policy was aimed partly at achieving higher yields and also reflected the need to have environmental impact assessments. The 1995 (later) White Paper heralded a five-year programme which emphasized the importance of liberalization of the internal gas and electricity supply markets, continuing availability of supply, and environmental protection, and various gas and electricity directives to introduce common rules for the internal market have followed. The 1996 Green Paper concentrated on renewable energy sources. In 1997 a master plan for the development of Trans-European Energy Networks was published, with the intention of widening access to energy grids. It was set against a background which is surprising to most of us: about 40 per cent of the EU's current energy needs are supplied from third countries (Norway, Russia and Algeria), and this figure is likely to rise to 60 per cent within ten years. The development of networks is expensive, and the European Investment Bank and the European Investment Fund are assisting in this area.

The third principle of Community energy policy is the impact of energy use and production on the environment. Energy and its production are no longer a national matter, or even a Community matter. It is of international interest, given the impact on third countries that energy production can have, both in economic and environmental terms. International discussions on the environment and emissions continue. At a joint energy/environmental council in 1990 it was agreed that the global Community carbon dioxide emissions would be stabilized at their 1990 levels by the year 2000. The Council set out measures to achieve this objective in 1995, and Guidelines on the reduction of Greenhouse Gases were produced in March 1998 with a further communication on a strategy relating to climatic change.

Energy policy is extremely important in the EU's relations with the EFTA countries under the EEA agreement, and with the countries of Eastern Europe and the CIS. The EC was one of the 51 signatories of the European Energy Charter in 1991, the aim of which was to trigger economic recovery in the former Soviet Union countries and Eastern Europe by a joint effort to develop the region's energy resources, modernize its energy industries and expand energy trade, as well as achieve security of supplies in Europe. The Energy Charter was linked to a Treaty of the Charter 1994 which sought to bind energy supply and trade to the WTO rules. It has not yet been ratified in all the signatory states.

The Community also have various incentives and programmes to develop alternative sources of non-polluting energy, to reinforce energy efficiency, on both the domestic and industrial fronts, to encourage energy conservation, and to promote more energy-efficient transport methods and infrastructures. These include R&D programmes such as Thermie (to promote innovative energy technologies); SAVE (to promote energy efficiency); and ALTENER (to promote renewable energy resources through supporting feasibility studies and research into the biomass market).

All these programmes are having an effect, but it is possibly the 'green' consumer who is urging national governments to greater, greener efforts, and who is, frankly, afraid of the effects of polluting energy producers, and long-term effects of, for example, Chenobyl-type disasters.

POLICIES FOR PEOPLE

Consumer protection policy

Consumer protection in the Community context is needed because in the Single Market where people live and work, and go on holiday in different Member countries, they are consumers in those countries, and it is important that their expectations as to their rights should be met, at least as to their most basic protections. This means there has to be a comprehensive body of Community legislation.

The way in which the area of consumer policy has developed in a Community context is interesting. While there has been a Community policy in relation to consumers since 1972, as it was recognized that consumers should have protection and some input into the decisions that affect them, it was not until the Single European Act 1986 that the principle of consumer protection was added by Article 100 to the Treaties, and the Consumer Policy Service was set up at Community level. The TEU in 1982 made consumer protection a Community Policy in its own right, and the Amsterdam Treaty 1997 goes further, requiring that consumer protection should be taken into account when defining and implementing other policies. This progression as to the perceived importance of the consumer lobby (and indeed the citizen as consumer) can also be seen in the significant raft of consumer legislation. This ranges from food labelling and unit pricing regulations, and the use of asbestos in consumer goods; to safety of household products and electrical goods. The wide range extends from the Toy Safety Directive preventing dangerous toys from being sold in the EU, to provisions to prevent dangerous imitations (eg erasers looking like sweets which could be swallowed by children); and controls on genetically modified organisms, the labelling of irradiated foods, and general marketing practices. It is certainly important, too, that consumers have enough information to enable them to compare prices and choose the goods they buy in an informed way. They have become used to expecting a degree of safety in what they buy.

Various action plans have been taken in this area, although it has frequently been argued that not enough funding is allocated to help Community consumer protection programmes. The activities have been targeted at encouraging, for example:

- better consumer information, and more recently, education
- better consumer protection and safety
- better cross-border payments systems
- better and cheaper access to justice
- more transparency in, eg tele-purchasing and financial services
- better health protection
- better consumer support activities.

There is also a drive to assist the development of consumer protection policies in the applicant countries of Central and Eastern Europe.

Some of the more important directives are listed below:

1. the Product Liability Directive 1985. This made manufacturers and importers strictly liable, subject to various defences for injuries caused by defective products. This does not extend to all goods sold: for example primary agricultural produce is excluded, although there is a proposal to include it.
2. General Product Safety Directive 1992. This placed a general duty on manufacturers to ensure that the goods they put on the market are safe, and carry the appropriate warnings and instructions. This also extends to liability for second-hand goods.
3. Consumer Credit Directives – there have been various directives in this regard to protect consumers by requiring harmonized methods of calculating APR, for example, and generally harmonizing national provisions.
4. Misleading Advertising Directive 1984. This aimed to protect consumers and businesses against the effects of misleading advertisements. It has been amended by the Comparative Advertising Directive 1997 which permits some comparisons to be made in advertising, subject to quite strict conditions. It should perhaps be noted that a total ban on tobacco advertising is currently going through, taking effect in phases until 2006.

5. the Doorstep Selling Directive 1985, more properly called the Directive on Sales away from Business Premises, provided for seven day cooling off periods for doorstep agreements which are for more than very small sums, to enable often pressurized consumers to cancel.
6. the Distance Selling Directive 1997 provides details of the minimum information which must be given for contracts made 'at a distance, eg through the post, mail order or via the TV or Teletext, and provides that goods should be delivered within 30 days, and details rights to refunds, etc. Financial services are covered by separate controls.
7. the Directive on Package Trips, Package Holidays, and Tours Put Up for Sale in the EC 1990 also sets out the minimum information which must be given, and the minimum consumer protection which must be offered.
8. the Unfair Contracts (or Abusive Terms) Directive 1993 outlawed the use of these clauses, ie which unfairly create an imbalance of rights as between the parties to the detriment of the consumer. This is a complicated area, and further information can be obtained either from the Department of Trade and Industry, or the Commission.

As may be seen, there are many strands to consumer protection, not least the need for consumers to have access to justice in other Member States, and this is a matter which is being addressed by the EU. There are now more than ten cross-border information centres which can give information as to access to courts, and the provisions of the Enforcement of Judgements (Brussels) Convention, and its sister the Lugano Convention do help considerably in this regard. The Commission's 'Guide to Legal Aid and Advice in the European Economic Area' which is also available on the Internet is invaluable. The Commission publishes various publications concerning Consumer Policy (see Appendix V page 151).

The Consumers in Europe Group is another useful source of information about Consumer Protection Policy in the EU, and also produce valuable publications. Their address is:
CEG Consumers in Europe Group,
20 Grosvenor Gardens,
London SW1W ODH
Telephone: 0171 881 3021 Fax: 0171 730 8540

Youth and education

For the majority of people, the most tangible sign of a Community without internal frontiers is the freedom of movement. The right to study, work and live in another country is something which our predecessors never enjoyed. The EU has launched several initiatives to make it easier for people in general, young workers, students, teachers and scientists to move around the Community.

The TEU included a new chapter entitled 'Education, Vocational Training and Youth' and, in recognition of the need to train up the well-equipped employees of the future so central to the success of the EU as a whole, committed the EU to having a vocational training policy. This has been carried forward in successive programmes.

The objectives set out in that chapter were:

● to develop the European dimension in education, particularly through the teaching and dissemination of the languages of the Member States
● to encourage the mobility of students and teachers, *inter alia* by encouraging the academic recognition of diplomas and periods of study
● to promote cooperation between educational establishments
● to develop exchanges of information and experience on issues common to the education systems of the Member States
● to encourage development of youth exchanges of socio-educational instructors
● to facilitate access to vocational training, to stimulate cooperation of training between educational or training establishments and to develop exchanges of information on issues common to the training systems of Member States.

Most recently the use of a 'Europass' to record work-related training which has been undertaken in another Member State, and is recognized as valid vocational training throughout the EU was agreed in June 1998.

The Youth for Europe III Programme 1995–99 is open to the 15 EU states, Iceland, Liechtenstein and Norway, and seeks to encourage the growth of exchanges for young people between the ages of 15 to 25. Its 5 action themes are as follows:

● Action A is aimed at young people currently outside formal education or training establishments to promote exchanges and placements in other Member States. It also supports voluntary work by young people in Member States other than their own which benefits the host country.
● Action B is targeted at support workers relating to Action A, to help them to develop skills to encourage young people in Europe, and to co-ordinate their training.

- Action C seeks to promote the development of partnerships leading to cooperation between relevant organizations in Member States which concern young people.
- Action D promotes exchanges between EU countries and many others including regions in Central and Eastern Europe, the Mediterranean and Latin America.
- Action E is to encourage the development of information and innovation exchange networks to encourage research and the sharing of information to enable young people to understand what the EU programmes have to offer.

Further information can be obtained from:
Joane Anthony,
Youth Exchange Centre,
The British Council,
10 Spring Gardens,
London SW1A 2BN
Telephone: 0171 389 4030 Fax: 0171 389 4033
e-mail: j.anthony@britcoun.org

As to the education sector – there are a number of programmes funded by the EU, and it should be noted that these are not grants or fees which can be applied for by individuals.

The largest programme is SOCRATES, and the current five-year programme started on 1 January 1995, and supports cross-border cooperation in schools and higher educational establishments in the EU. It incorporates various programmes, for example:

1. SOCTRATES–ERASMUS for higher education which promotes European integration in universities largely to enable students to study for a minimum of three months in another Member State as part of the degree or academic qualification. Over 1600 universities and 200 000 students will be participating in the 1998/9 Erasmus programme in the higher education sector.
   Further information is available from:

The Socrates–Erasmus Council,
The Research and Development Building,
The University of Kent,
Canterbury CT2 7PD
Tel: 01227 762 712 Fax: 01227 762 711
e-mail: erasmus@ukc.ac.uk

or Socrates Erasmus Bureau,
70 rue Montoyer,
B1949 Brussels
Tel:(322) 233 0111.

2. SOCRATES–COMENIUS for school education. This has two action
strands: Action 1 requires a partnership between at least three schools in
three Member States, and develops one or more subject areas of European interest through a set of activities integrated into the normal school
activities. It encourages foreign language teaching, and the exchange of
information relating to teaching and new methods.
Action 2 is geared at improving the schooling of migrant workers, with
inter-cultural teaching practices as a significant part.
Further information on both areas can be obtained from:

The British Council,
Central Bureau for Educational Visits and Exchanges,
10 Spring Gardens,
London SW1A 2BN
Tel: 0171 389 4021 Fax: 0171 389 4426
e-mail: jnilsson@centralbureau.org.uk (Action 1)
e-mail poudjanus@centralbureau.org.uk (Action 2)

3. SOCRATES–LINGUA aims to promote and develop language skills in
Europe, and is largely aimed at improving the training and teaching
methods of teachers. It also encourages cross-border student exchanges
between two or more schools.
Further information is available from Angela Shakleton at the British
Council at the above address. Tel: 0171 389 4840. Fax 0171 389 4426.
e-mail: ashakleton@centralbureau.org.uk

or The Socrates Lingua Bureau,
Rue de Commerce,
B1040 Brussels
Tel: (322) 511 4218.

4. SOCRATES–ARION concerns cooperation in respect of educational
theory, and again information is available from:

The British Council,
Central Bureau for Educational Visits and Exchanges,
10 Spring Gardens,
London SW1A 2BN
Tel: 0171 389 4629 Fax 0171 389 4426
e-mail: degeue@centralbureau.org.uk

5. SOCRATES–EURYDICE concerns the exchange of information on the structures and organization of educational systems in Member States, and information may be obtained from:

Socrates-Euridece,
15 Rue d'Arlon,
1050 Brussels
Tel: 0032 2 238 3011 Fax 0032 2 2380 6562

Other educational programmes include:

6. The TEMPUS programme to facilitate cooperation between higher education institutes to cooperate with their Central and Eastern European and COI (Commonwealth of Independent States) counterparts. Information may be obtained from:

The UK Tempus Information Office,
Research and Development Building,
The University of Kent,
Canterbury CT2 7PD
Tel: 01227 824 067 Fax 01227 824 468
e-mail: tempus uk@ukc.ac.uk

or from the European Training Foundation,

Villa Gualino 65, Viale Settimo Severo,
10133 Turin,
Italy
Tel: 0039 11 630 2222 Fax: 0039 11 630 2200
e-mail: tempus@ets.it

7. The LEONARDO DA VINCI five-year action programme which also started on the 1 January 1995, relating to vocational training supersedes a number of other programmes (eg PETRA, EUROTECNET and FORCE). It includes a number of areas for action, and is aimed at encouraging EU-wide alliances with placements and exchanges in the different Member States.

There are various information points available on the Leonardo project including:

For joint ventures and work placements:

Ann Kinsella
The Central Bureau for Educational Visits and exchanges at the British Council,
Tel: 0171 389 4389/4509 Fax 0171 389 4426
e-mail: akinsella.centralbureau.org.uk

For vocational development:
Dave Saunders,
Department for Education and Employment,
Moorfoot,
Sheffield S1 4PQ
Tel: 0114 259 4502 Fax 0114 259 6985
e-mail: david.saunders@dfee.gov.uk

Language skill development and cooperation:
John Goodwin,
Department of Education and Employment,
Level 4,
Caxton House,
Tothill Street,
London SW1H 9NF
Tel: 0171 273 5660 Fax 0171 273 5475
e-mail: etp@depemp.demon.co.uk

General information may be obtained from:
Leonardo da Vinci Information,
Duilio Silletti,
DG22 B/1,
rue Delliard,
1049 Brussels
Tel: 0032 2295 72 02 Fax 0032 22 95 5704
e-mail: leonardo@dg22.cec.be

The European Commission Representation in the UK has produced a useful booklet *Background Report on European Educational Integration and Student Grants* from which this information has been taken, and provides details also of other related programmes and funding, together with details of where to obtain further information.

Travelling and working in Europe

The free movement of workers was guaranteed in Article 48 of the Treaty of Rome, although there is a public policy exception, which has to be restrictively interpreted. This means that every EU national as a citizen of the EU can in principle move freely around the EU to live and work provided he or she complies with any relevant local requirements, and can take their spouse or usual partner and dependent family with him or her. In fact under 2 per cent of the working age population in EU Member States are from other EU countries. There are various directives setting out the provisions, and as the position can be complicated, the Commission has issued a series of guidance publications under its Citizens First information campaign, and these are available on request to a Freephone number: 0800 581 591 to inform citizens about their rights. It should be noted that almost all the rights which are enjoyed by EU nationals in the 15 Member States may also apply in the extra countries which belong to the EEA, ie Iceland, Norway and Liechtenstein, and to their nationals wishing to work in the EU.

Most of us have probably travelled to somewhere in another Member State on holiday, and have enjoyed the lack of formalities, albeit the UK and Ireland retain their border checks in the interest of preventing illegal immigration, terrorist activity, drug running and rabies control. The other EU countries have progressively removed internal border checks under an agreement called the Schengen Agreement, which is being incorporated into the EU's single institutional framework under the Amsterdam Treaty. It will also be applied in Iceland and Norway who are part of the Nordic Passport Union.

It is interesting, and may be useful to know that if you are a national of one of the Member States of the EU, and you have a problem in a country in which your own country has no consular representation, then you can request assistance from an embassy or consulate of any Member State which is there.

One of the results of having open borders is the need to have greater cooperation between national police forces, and this has been progressing, helped partly by the development of the Schengen Information System, and the institution of EUROPOL, the European Police Office based in The Hague which has the remit of facilitating police cooperation and information exchange to prevent or combat drug trafficking, terrorism and various other forms of international crime.

So much for travelling in Europe, but what about going to work in another EU country?

It is fine to have community-wide information networks such as EURES (European Employment Services) to help you find a job elsewhere in the EU, and to give information about the job markets in Europe (there are over 450 Eurocounsellors in the EU who are trained to advise and find job placements for those seeking work in another Member State who can be contacted through your local Job Centre) but what are your rights as an EU citizen? You are entitled to apply for jobs across the EU, and to be recruited under the same conditions as nationals of that country. You can apply for any job, provided it is not within the exceptions, ie retained for nationals only by reasons of security, or eg in the armed forces. You can also register with local job agencies.

Of course you also have to know about recognition of qualifications. Over the years there have been problems with ensuring acceptance and recognition of degrees, diplomas and other professional qualifications gained in other Member States, and there has been a progression of directives to ensure that artificial barriers are not put up to prevent people carrying on their professional activities in a second country, and the situation has become easier. Thus if you are an architect, doctor, dentist, general nurse, midwife, veterinary surgeon or pharmacist, your qualification is automatically recognized in all the Member States. If you are a physiotherapist, accountant, lawyer, engineer or teacher, then although your qualification will be recognized, you may be required to undergo additional training or experience. If the profession is unregulated in the host country, then no formal recognition is needed before practising it.

If you wish to set up a business in another EU country, then you have to consider the local provisions, albeit the Treaty of Rome provided for the freedom of establishment stating that within the framework of the Treaty provisions, restrictions on the freedom of establishment of nationals of one Member State in the territory of another Member State should be abolished by progressive stages. This also applied to restrictions on the setting up of agencies, branches or subsidiaries by nationals of any Member State who are already established in another Member State, so you can also carry out activities as a self-employed person, or set up and manage undertakings, for example companies or firms (including co-operatives) which have been legally formed in, and have their registered office, administration or principal place of business in another Member State. In other words, nationals of one Member State, ie individuals, and this includes legal persons, ie legally formulated enterprises, are entitled to take up and follow a profession or occupation or carry out a business in any other Member State. There are still differences which have to be watched for, but they are not insuperable.

It is important to get good local legal advice before setting up, as otherwise you can have unpleasant surprises, for example in the distribution sector, where there are no common rules as such. This means that a distributorship may be governed by provisions totally different to those in the home country of the manufacturer. Also in some countries there are some unexpected requirements, for example in Belgium everyone, Belgians and non-Belgians, must obtain special permission to open department stores, provide transportation services, produce or sell certain food items, or cut or polish diamonds, or sell firearms or ammunition.

As to social security rights – these vary too, and various directives ensure a measure of protection but again local advice is needed. Even if you are unemployed you have a right to go and live in another EU country to look for a job, but your time of residence there may be restricted unless you can prove that you are genuinely looking for employment, but you must be careful to ensure you do not lose entitlement to your unemployment or other benefits (if any).

There are special provisions relating to students, researchers and academics and trainees moving around Europe with regard to maintenance grants, etc and you should check these.

If you are thinking of retiring to a different EU country, then again special provisions apply, and advice should be sought.

Employment with the EU's institutions

Competition to work for the EU institutions is keen in many countries of the EU, and it is surprising that this is not so in the UK, which is still under-represented on their staff in Brussels, Luxembourg and Strasbourg. Because this has been recognized as a problem here the UK government has been supporting an information drive to ensure that UK nationals know more about the challenging and interesting work that is available, and so they set up the European Staffing Division, which gives advice and practical assistance at each stage of the recruitment process to UK applicants.

The Stagiaire scheme

There is also a Stagiaire scheme whereby, for periods of between three and five months, candidates with a second language who have a degree and may be from the universities or the private or public sectors may apply to take in-service trainee posts with the EU institutions. I did this in 1973, and can vouch for the fact that it is a very valuable experience as it enables trainees to gain a better insight into the workings of the EU, and incidentally to make friends from other parts of the EU. There are about 200 places a year, and it is not easy to obtain a place, and candidates have to apply about six months in advance of their intended stage period. Information can be obtained from the UK Commission Representation Office, or from DGIX, Training Division, European Commission, 200 rue de la Loi, B-1049 Brussels. There is a similar opportunity at the European Parliament Secretariat via the Robert Schuman Scholarships. Information for these is available from: Robert Schuman Scholarships, European Parliament, Schuman Building, Luxembourg.

The European recruitment competitions or 'concours' are held periodically, and a useful information booklet has been produced and that, together with further information is available from:
The European Staffing Division,
Office of Public Service,
Horse Guards Road,
London SW1P 3AL
Tel: 0171 270 6312
e-mail: euro.staff@gtnet.gov.uk

MONEY MATTERS

The Community budget

Over the lifetime of the Community there have been considerable changes in the way in which revenue has been raised. Initially the Community's budget was dependent upon contributions by the Member States according to their relative wealth. Later the Community was able to raise its revenue through duties on imports into the EC and by a percentage of all VAT receipts in the Community. This is known as the Community's 'own resources' system.

One of the most important issues in the Community in the early 1980s was the level of contribution of the UK to the EC budget. This debate has been well documented. A long-term solution to the budget debate was agreed at the Fontainebleau Summit in 1984. Now the Community budget is limited to a sliding scale of 1.20 per cent of the Gross National Product (GNP) of all Member States in 1996, rising to 1.27 per cent of GNP in 1999. The 1998 budget of the EU totals ECU90.9 billion in commitments, and for the first time included Common Foreign and Security Policy. The projections for 1999–2006 totals ECU275 billion, to include reservations of ECU45 billion for the Central and East European countries scheduled to join the EU.

The arguments now centre not on the size of the budget, but around how it is spent, and there continues to be resentment about the proportion of funds devoted to the Common Agricultural Policy (CAP) and EAGGF Guarantees. In 1996 this was 48 per cent of the whole budget, which compares well with the 59 per cent expended in 1988, and 80.6 per cent in 1973 but is still felt to be too much, considering the urban and industrial problems within the EU, so further reforms in this area are being made. Having said this, it cannot be disputed that the success of the EC's CAP is real, as it has improved efficiency and prevented shortages of food. However, it has also created volumes of surplus production which was costly to dispose of. Thus reforms have centred on reducing support prices and encouraging higher quality rather than quantity, setting quotas in areas such as milk and encouraging set aside.

In 1996, the next largest slice at 31 per cent of the budget was taken by structural operations to support greater economic and social cohesion in the regions of the Member States, and the sum to be spent in this area is set to rise to ECU34.6 billion in 1999 (at 1997 prices) following the Edinburgh agreement to assist the development of the poorest regions and the conversion of the declining industrial regions; to combat long-term unemployment and social exclusion, to help workers to adjust to industrial change, to promote rural development, to modernize agricultural and fisheries structures in general through the Structural Funds (see Part IV on regional policies and Structural Funds).

Other significant percentages of the budget are taken up with external actions, Research and Development programmes, the European Coal and Steel Community support costs, other internal policy costs, the European Development Fund, and smallest of all, administration costs.

Determining the size and shape of the budget is a complex process. It starts with a draft prepared by the Commission. This takes into account expenditure already committed or expected, probable income, and the guidelines and priorities laid down by the Council and the European Parliament. Like every national budget, it must make a series of calculated bets on such matters as food prices, the values of currencies, changes in earning power, and international events. Once agreed by the Commission, it is put to the Council for lengthy debate, and invariably amendment. Once the Council has adopted the revised draft it goes to the European Parliament, who may propose modifications in some areas, and amend others. It usually has a relatively rough passage.

The European Parliament, who has to approve the budget, also has the right to reject the whole budget – a power exercised several times because it disagreed both with its overall size and the priorities for expenditure awarded by the Council. The EP uses its powers as a political lever; in some senses its most positive achievement has been to establish machinery for the resolution of budgetary conflict between the Commission and the Council. The EP is also a valuable ally of the Court of Auditors in keeping a close eye on how the money is actually spent, and whether the Commission has monitored this properly.

Fraud is a problem, and there is now a free confidential hotline number in each Member State for citizens who wish to give details of any suspicions they may have. In the UK the anti-fraud hotline is 0800 96 35 95.

The European Monetary System (EMS) and the drive towards European Monetary Union (EMU)

The European Monetary System was launched on 5 December 1978 and came into operation on 13 March 1979. It was intended to achieve monetary stability and engender cooperation and convergence of economic policy and performance in the Member States. It has four main areas:

- the Exchange Rate Mechanism (ERM)
- the European Currency Unit (ECU)
- the European Monetary Cooperation Fund (EMCF) and
- the Very Short-term Financing Facility (VSTF).

The UK left the ERM in 1992 due to currency difficulties and has not yet rejoined. In the same year the Member States agreed the Treaty on European Union, and as a significant part of the TEU agreed to adopt a single currency and European Monetary Union (EMU). There were two protocols which enabled the UK and Denmark to opt out if they so wish. In 1993 the participating countries agreed to keep their currencies within a fluctuation band extended to between +/- 15 per cent. Under the TEU it was agreed that in order for a Member State to join EMU they must first comply with the convergence criteria, which included that they should have remained within the normal fluctuation bands of the EMS for at least two years, limits as to acceptable inflation, control of government deficits, and a limit on long-term interest rates.

EMU was to be achieved in three stages:

1. Stage 1 (which pre-dated the TEU) abolished capital controls by Member States.
2. Stage 2 started at the beginning of 1994 and ran through to 1997 during which time Member States were required to bring their economic performances into line with the best performing Member States (known as 'convergence'). The poorer countries, Greece, Ireland, Portugal and Spain, were assisted financially through a new fund, the 'Cohesion Fund'. A new institution, the European Monetary Institute (EMI) was set up to prepare the institutional arrangements for Stage 3 of EMU.
3. the timetable for Stage 3 (the move to a single currency) slipped a bit, but it was confirmed in 1995 that it should start on 1 January 1999.

see —1 other book pg 153 Maastricht

It has now been agreed that the Member States who have complied (some would say that a little bit of cheating has been going on) with the convergence criteria will be part of the Single Currency as of 1 January 1999. Eleven Member States are scheduled to be participants, ie all the Member States except the UK and Denmark (which both had 'opt outs' under the Treaty and had decided not to join at this time but may decide to join later); and Greece and Sweden, neither of which have met the criteria.

On 1 January 1999 the European Central Bank (ECB) will replace the EMI, take over the management of the currency reserves of participating Member States and manage the currency; and will deal with the single monetary policy.

The Stability and Growth Pact of June 1997 sought to ensure a continuation of convergence after 1 January 1999 which is the date agreed as the start of the changeover to the Euro (the new currency) for those countries proceeding to EMU. These are: Austria, Belgium, Finland, France, Germany, Ireland, Italy, Luxembourg, Netherlands, Portugal and Spain. Thus Denmark, Greece, Sweden and the UK will remain outside the Euro area for the time being. In the Euro area the currency value of existing coins and notes will be fixed to that of the Euro from 1 January 1999, and they will be part of the Euro as currency, but actual Euro notes and coins will not be available until 1 January 2002 as the sheer production exercise is formidable.

Finally, it should be noted that the European Central Bank (ECB) has been set up and will become fully operational on 1 January 1999. It will be responsible for maintaining currency price stability and will define, in cooperation with the European System of Central Banks (ESCB) which comprises the Governors of all the participating Central Banks, the general economic and monetary policy which the national central banks will implement, albeit the relevant Ministers in the Council will set the exchange rate policy for the Euro zone.

Like it or not, the UK, its citizens and businesses will be affected by the Euro area. Businesses in particular will have to compete with Euro zone firms tendering for contracts and supplying goods to other countries in the Euro area which do not have to include the extra currency conversion expenses included in their own costings. On the plus side, the Euro should be a more stable currency than that of the various individual countries. It will be interesting to see how the transparency which will follow the institution of the single currency will lead to changes in the social security and wage structures in the EU as a whole. The current UK Government has made it clear that it feels that the UK should join the Euro zone if EMU is successful, and the economic arguments become clear and unambiguous in its favour. Many believe recent events in the US, Russia and Japan, and the freefall of financial markets have again threatened the success, and possibly even the start, of the Euro zone. Time will tell.

It is important that both businesses and citizens understand the changes, and indeed know how to deal with any changes which may affect them. The UK Treasury has produced useful fact sheets particularly for businesses which may be obtained by telephoning: 08456 01 01 99, or by accessing their website: (http://www.euro.gov.uk). These include advice and details as to where you can go for further information in the UK and in the different EU countries. The Commission and its website and EIOs have useful information, as does the Bank of England and individual TECs, Chambers of Commerce and other professional and trade organizations.

Taxation

The situation with regard to taxation in the EU is becoming increasingly complicated, and it is impossible to cover it all here, but it is helpful to know the following. The Treaty of Rome provided for the progressive approximation of the economic policies of the Member States, and Articles 95–100 concern taxation; and the harmonization of taxation across the Community was felt to be essential for the creation of a Single Market.

The Treaty on European Union (TEU) amended Articles 99 and 100 to strengthen the powers of the Council with regard to harmonization and approximation of legislation concerning turnover taxes, excise duties and other forms of indirect taxation necessary to ensure the establishment and functioning of the Internal Market. In assessing the Community's tax problems, it was important to examine not only the level, but also the composition of total taxation, ie the relative weights of direct and indirect taxation.

Direct taxation refers to the taxes which are imposed directly on individuals or firms; it includes, for example, personal income tax, corporation tax, inheritance tax, etc.

In the case of indirect taxation, the taxes are included in the price of goods or services and are therefore borne by the final consumer. The breakdown of the tax burden as between direct and indirect taxes varies widely from one country to another in the Community. Trying to reconcile these widely disparate tax approaches has so far been a lengthy business. Partly this has been for the obvious reason that sovereignty in tax matters, which is basic to the democratic process, is regarded as a fundamental prerogative of national parliaments. Partly it has been because tax adjustments have proved an indispensable national weapon during periods of economic crisis.

However, the Council formally recognized in 1996 that a comprehensive approach to tax policy would make a considerable contribution to the development of intra-EU trade, to growth and employment, and could assist the environment. Work continues to achieve the existing aims: to harmonize VAT, excise and other indirect taxes to ensure a level playing field in taxation terms throughout the EU. There have been considerable improvements, and various VAT directives mean that VAT is now assessed on a uniform basis, with agreed rules for reimbursing tax to non-residents, arrangements for second-hand goods, provisions as to minimum rates, and simplification of VAT regimes. There have also been provisions to facilitate cross-border mutual assistance to seek to avoid fraudulent evasion of VAT.

As to excise duties: a 1992 Council Directive introduced approximation of excise rates and provisions relating to various goods, eg alcohol, tobacco, and essential oils and as to bonded warehouses. Further legislation on duties includes that on petroleum products and biofuels which takes environmental aspects into consideration and encourages the use of fuels of agricultural origin (Directive of June 1996).

As to direct taxes: there have been considerable changes in the 1990s. In 1993 a recommendation was issued concerning direct taxation to encourage the achievement of fiscal equality for residents to encourage mobility of labour, and there are various bilateral Conventions, and ECJ decisions in this regard. Corporate tax provisions relate to parent and subsidiary companies in different Member States, capital movements, and transfer pricing. Disputes do arise particularly with regard to corporate taxation, and so the Arbitration Convention came into effect on 1 January 1995 to assist taxing authorities in different Member States to come to agreement where problems arise and to prevent double taxation.

SMEs cause particular problems, and the Commission has issued guidelines to encourage a situation whereby the provisions should be simplified to avoid dual taxation, and to make SMEs taxable only in their place of registered office.

It is suggested that the advent of European Monetary Union in 11 Member States as from 1 January 1999 will make a difference, as will the efforts being made to harmonize accounting practices throughout the EU.

Competition Policy

This important area of EC activity is highly complex, affecting many areas, from public procurement to patents and trade marks. I define it as the policy aimed at seeking through legislation, decisions and actions, to control anti-competitive practices, particularly the abuse of dominant positions in the market place; and to simultaneously seek to improve the competitiveness of the EU. Thus monopolies, mergers, state aid, and potentially anti-competitive agreements and practices in a Community context have to be policed, and offenders penalized.

Most of the Commission's powers are derived from Articles 85 (prohibition of concerted practices), 84 (abuse of a dominant position) and 90 of the Rome Treaty. These have been construed and extended by case law, and indeed by legislation. The EC rules are mirrored in the EEA agreement, so EC competition provisions extend throughout the EEA countries.

Competition provisions should be marked 'for comment and explanation by experts only', but may be useful to bear in mind. If you think you are being adversely affected by the abuse of a significant dominant position you may be able to make a proper complaint to the Commission, who may take up the issue. The Office of Fair Trading is a useful source of information as is the Commission's Competition Directorate.

Part VI

Developing Europe

REGIONAL POLICIES IN THE EU AND CONVERGENCE

The economic and social differences in the Member States have always been there, and are of immense importance, particularly in the context of European Monetary Union. The Community has long worked to improve the situation in the poorer states, and there were fears that the Single Market would exacerbate the situation.

The drive towards economic convergence has therefore been continuing for many years, largely through a system of support in the form of non-repayable grants, usually with matching government or local authority support, for poorer regions, hopefully structured in such a way as to enable them to become net contributors in their turn. Ireland is a useful example of how assistance has primed the economy, and will no longer qualify for some of the Structural Funding.

To fund these grants, and other budget lines and expenses, the EU collects a maximum of 1.24 per cent (in 1996) of the VAT revenue of individual Member States, which also give a maximum of 1.22 per cent (in 1996) of their Gross National Product (GNP) to the EU, which also collects customs duties from non-EU countries goods imported into the EU. These funds are then used to support the various expenses and funds of the EU.

There are four Structural Funds of the EU:

1. the European Regional Development Fund (ERDF)
2. the European Social Fund (ESF)
3. the European Agricultural Guidance and Guarantee Fund (EAGGF)
4. the Financial Instrument for Fisheries Guidance (FIFG).

THE EUROPEAN REGIONAL DEVELOPMENT FUND (ERDF)

This provides assistance to create or maintain jobs, infrastructure, and TENs (in Objective 1 regions – see below) for assistance for training, and education for business and economic development, for R&D and environmental projects. It has a wide remit, with various programmes run under it, examples of which are given below.

THE EUROPEAN SOCIAL FUND (ESF)

This should not be confused with the UK concept of 'social' in terms of voluntary work for which there are virtually no Community monies available. Articles 123–127 of the Treaty of Rome outlined the objectives of the Social Fund – to render employment of workers easier and to increase their geographical mobility in order to contribute to raising the standards of living in the Member States. The ESF itself was therefore set up in 1960 to improve employment opportunities by providing financial support for vocational training schemes, to improve workers' capabilities in scientific fields, to help job creation and job stability measures, and to assist with educational and training systems. The key priorities for 1994–99 are:

- to combat long-term unemployment and to assist young people into work (eg Youthstart)
- to help people subject to exclusion in the job market
- to promote equal opportunities for men and women
- to support workers adapting to industrial change.

The fund is also used to support the Community Initiative on Employment and the Development of Human Resources (1994–99). Thus, for example, the ESF will assist projects to help women back to work, or disabled people, ethnic minorities or other disadvantaged groups, as well as those helping young people under 25 who have never worked, into the workplace.

The UK receives the largest grant of all the Member States from this fund. It should be noted, however, that as with other Structural Funds, applications for grant aid for projects should be routed through the appropriate government departments.

THE EUROPEAN AGRICULTURAL GUIDANCE AND GUARANTEE FUND (EAGGF)

The European Agricultural Guidance and Guarantee Fund was set up in 1962. Set against the background that the Agriculture and Fisheries Guarantees Section Fund in 1995 accounted for around 50 per cent of the EU budget, mostly going to guarantee farm prices and storage costs, the EAGGF Guidance Section is aimed at modernizing farming communities. It supports viable and hill farms, young farmers, farm efficiency, improvements in terms of quality, operation and marketing, rural infrastructures, rural tourism, woodland and heritage protection, and many other related initiatives.

THE FINANCIAL INSTRUMENT FOR FISHERIES GUIDANCE (FIFG)

This fund supports the regulation of fishing, quotas, development of fish farming, improvement of ports, promotion and improvement of fisheries products and marketing, and provides assistance to fishermen and fishing communities suffering from restructuring in their industry. It also promotes modernization of vessels and fleet reductions.

Since 1993 the Structural Funds have operated in a coordinated way through multi-annual programmes to carry out projects that come under essentially seven priority objectives, that seem to be more aimed at specific problems needing attention, rather than 'poor region' based as previously:

1. Objective 1: to develop regions lagging behind the EU average in terms of prosperity
2. Objective 2: to assist regions experiencing industrial decline
3. Objective 3: to help areas with long-term unemployment, or (anywhere) the young unemployed, or those suffering from social exclusion
4. Objective 4: to assist people to adapt to changes in industry and production systems (anywhere)
5. Objective 5a: to assist with modernization of agricultural and fisheries sectors
6. Objective 5b: to assist in the redevelopment of rural areas.
7. Objective 6: to assist areas with low populations (eg the Nordic states).

The present Structural Funds resources for 1994–99 are over ECU140bn.

The ERDF also funds innovative actions to encourage cooperation in the EU under Article 10, and ECU400m have been allocated for the years 1995–99 under its four categories. One example of such an action is RECITE.

REGIONS AND CITIES OF EUROPE (RECITE) AND RECITE II (1997–99)

The Community has been supporting direct cooperation between cities and regions in the various Member States since 1989. The first launch of the Regions and Cities of Europe Programme supported 36 inter-regional cooperation projects and networks of regional and local authorities across the EU in various fields, such as IT and technology transfer, economic development, assistance for SMEs, transport, rural development, education and training and social exclusion. The objectives of RECITE II are listed as:

1. to encourage the rapid transfer of know-how particularly from more advanced to less advanced regions
2. to stimulate cooperation based on joint projects and in response to shared problems and challenges
3. to promote the efficiency of administrations particularly those facing regional development problems in lagging regions
4. to encourage the development of Community policies particularly where then have an impact on regional development.

It should be noted that there are also various programmes emanating as special measures following Community Initiatives and these include YOUTHSTART (to help youth employment), KONVER (to help areas affected by a reduction in the defence industry), PESCA (to help areas affected by the restructuring of the fishing industry), RETEX (to help diversification of activities in declining textile industry areas), ADAPT (to help workers to adapt to industrial change) and URBAN (revitalization of depressed urban areas) as well as INTERREG II (1994–99) which has two aims: to develop cross-border cooperation to help border areas, and some coastal areas facing difficulties due to their isolation from their national economies; and in developing energy networks.

GETTING MONEY FROM EUROPE: GENERAL ADVICE ON APPLYING FOR HELP OR GETTING FUNDING FROM THE EU

A distinction should be made between the Structural and Cohesive funds and the Framework Programme funds, and it is suggested that careful research and good advice be taken before applying as this can make all the difference.

As a rule, the Community's financial contribution does not exceed half the total cost of the project, and may be as low as 25 per cent. But 100 per cent funding is possible when the Commission has an exclusive interest in the project concerned. If research, for example, is later exploited, then part of the Community grant may be repayable. All these details are made clear in detail on application forms enclosed with tender notices.

As a rule of thumb, before submitting an application for Community funding you should be able to show that your proposal:

- has a transnational character, involving collaboration between organizations in two or more Member States where this is required under a specific programme
- conforms with the general aims of the Community, eg if it is within one of the framework programmes
- has a good chance of eventual commercial success or 'Communautaire' value
- is neither open-ended research or 'blue skies' research, but will result in publishable results, if research, or another useful outcome.

In research in particular, two sectors are often directly involved: research and educational institutes in universities or colleges and government-funded agencies, on the one hand, and industrial companies, on the other. In the context of the competitiveness and the drive to create jobs, links between these sectors is being actively encouraged by the EU. Another aspect of collaborative research is to make possible large-scale projects which individual Member States may be unable or unwilling to finance themselves.

It is useful to note the availability of the European Economic Interest Grouping (EEIG) as a structure (a little like a form of partnership) which is being increasingly used where collaborative projects in research and development are being undertaken.

Funding from the Community can assist in such diverse areas as helping to restore a house of cultural and historic interest, to producing a multicultural television presentation, and some, such as Research and Development funding, have been covered elsewhere in this book. However, there are some principles which are common to all applications for funding within the EU. Although there is provision to help places affected by disasters through, for example the European Community Humanitarian Aid Office, in general, Community grants and assistance have nothing to do with charity. A policy for the regions is important to the aims of the Community, not only to level out the differences in employment, prosperity and opportunity between the various areas of Europe, but also to make the Community work more effectively. Help for small firms is not merely a salute to courage and entrepreneurship; it is based on the belief that the key to maintaining world competitiveness and jobs often lies with the SMEs.

Social policy is shaped partly by the decent, idealistic preamble to the Treaty of Rome, partly by economic realism. The European Social fund helps the handicapped, working women and migrant workers. Otherwise it has virtually nothing to offer for what we in the UK think of as social work. It is a training and re-training fund, aimed at filling jobs, and where possible helping to create them. It is an attack upon unemployment (particularly among the unskilled and disadvantaged), launched for hard-nosed, political reasons.

Generally, it is pointless to apply for any form of Community grant without the blessing of the UK government or one of its agencies. Those who seek grants from the EU have everything to gain by keeping in close touch with Community officials. However, there is no short-circuiting government channels; there is, however, a difference between approaching a national civil servant dealing with loans and grants, and his counterpart in the Commission. The latter will often be frank and informative in a fashion which is astonishing the first time you encounter it.

Another point to be made forcibly is that Community aid policies are far from static. Priorities change, sometimes suddenly, and terms and conditions can be flexible. Knowing when to ask for money can be as important as knowing whether its worth asking for it at all. Here personal contacts with UK or Commission officials and MEPs can pay real dividends. More recently there has been a mushrooming of EU consultancy agencies, in Brussels and most capitals of EU states offering this sort of information – but be wary. Some do not deliver, and great care must be taking in checking out consultants before you take them on or pay them. Much of the information may be available easily through, for example TED, and what you need will be extra expertise.

Finally, if necessary, ask again. This is one of the most important and least appreciated aspects of Community aid.

To sum up: if you seek money from Europe in the forms of grants, remember:

- all Community grants are work-related in one way or another
- you must normally have a UK department on your side

- make and maintain contacts in the Commission and among MEPs but don't try to upstage UK civil servants, who generally know the game better than you do
- remember the importance of timing: take experienced advice
- don't give up at the first refusal.

ADDITIONALITY

The question of additionality has been aired at length in the UK press and television but without much illumination. The word is shorthand for the assumption, implicit in EC regional policy, that aid from the various Community sources should be additional to that given by the government of the country concerned. It should be additional money, creating jobs, or training opportunities; or roads or bridges or dams that a national government would otherwise have been unable to afford.

A publicist for Community aid would clearly be delighted if Community grants went direct to companies in particular areas for a clearly identified purpose which would create a quantified number of jobs. But would this be sensible or even feasible? The staff of the Regional Development Fund, covering so many countries and regions and thousands of different problems would fit comfortably into one corner of one floor of one building of the UK Department of Trade and Industry. How could a few officials based in Brussels possibly adjudicate between the thousands of very different claims upon Community funds – between, say, a water scheme in Fife, a gas pipeline in France, or a road bridge in Italy – without relying on expert local and government advice? However, priorities will very often coincide. The EC therefore puts its money into those projects which national and local administrators and experts consider to be particularly important and timely.

Community grants (even small ones) can have a useful pump priming effect. There are several enterprise trusts and local initiatives which have managed to gather large resources of money, effort, time and equipment from private industry, local authorities and quangos for job creation and training, and which would never have got off the ground without the initial backing of Community funds.

Two things are definite about the use of European money in the UK. The first is that the UK government honours, and has honoured the concept of additionality in both the spirit and the letter as honestly and effectively as any other Community government; and appears at its most acquisitive in, for example, the use it makes of the Social Fund to finance ongoing training schemes. The end result is still of direct benefit to UK citizens. This book is not the place to plug the value of Community aid to the UK, but it is surely acceptable to say that the UK has had at least its fair share of such aid, and has earned international respect for the ways in which it has been used.

Finally, the amount of information available concerning grants and how to apply for them is mind-boggling, but the sources of information are there. The booklet which has been invaluable in compiling the information in this chapter is entitled *Funding from the European Union* in the European Information series, is published by the Representation of the European Commission in the United Kingdom in conjunction with NatWest, and is available free of charge from the Commission's information offices. There are also databases, listed at the end of this book, and the Commission publications produced by the UK representation can be consulted on the Internet: (http://www.cec.org.uk).

PUBLIC PROCUREMENT – CONTRACTS AND TENDERS

Every day millions of pounds are up for grabs in new contracts for public works, public supply, public utilities and public services contract, ie public procurement contracts. These are of vital importance to most big businesses in the Western world, and of increasing interest to SMEs. Since many of these contracts are not awarded by national governments but by regional and local authorities, the amount at stake as a whole is difficult to assess. A Commission estimate in 1986 put the total at about 9 per cent of Gross Domestic Product (GDP) in the Communities. By 1996 this estimate had risen to 11.5 per cent of GDP in the enlarged Community. This means billions of pounds.

All firms established in the Community have, in theory, the right to compete on equal terms (with a few strictly defined exceptions) for all relevant public procurement contracts. But some have proved to be more equal than others, and both national governments and local authorities have found ways of bending the rules, or not applying them correctly, despite the Public Purchasing Remedies Directive 1989 (sometimes referred to as the 'Compliance Directive') which was amended by the Services Directive 1992, and the Utilities Remedies Directive 1992, all of which were designed to prevent breaches of the rules. It is possible to complain about unfairness or contest the award of a contract by writing to the Commission, which may take the offending party before the ECJ. In this area particularly, state aids tend to cause unfairness, and the competition provisions may provide useful ammunition.

The provisions relating to public procurement are complicated, and the provisions are divided to cover the particular areas. The Commission's Green Paper 1997 is useful to read in that it reviews progress in this area, and underlines its intention of making sure that all public contracts come within a definition. The 1993 Directive on Public Works Contracts governs large projects such as engineering projects, and relates to public works contracts including those projects with at least 50 per cent public funding and valued at over ECU5m. The Public Supply Contract Directive 1993 governs rental, lease, purchase or hire purchase of goods worth more than ECU200,000 (unless the contract is also governed by the WTO agreement on government procurement, in which case the thresholds may be different). This directive set out three kinds of tendering procedure:

- open: whereby anyone can apply
- restricted: whereby applications must be pre-vetted
- negotiated: chosen contractors only may apply.

In practice, many procedures are open, although the UK favours the restricted procedure.

Public utilities (energy, transport, water, and telecommunications) supply contracts are regulated by the Excluded Sector Directive 1990, often referred to as 'the Utilities Directive', They also cover privatized industries because of the political influence to which they may be subject.

Contracts which are not classified as contracts for public works or supplies are generally public services contracts, and usually have to have a bid value of over ECU200,000 (unless they concern architects' fees, in which case they usually relate to construction contracts, and a ECU5m threshold applies). This can include services as diverse as advertising and sewage disposal.

Those putting out (and indeed putting in for) large public tenders do not only have to take account of EU provisions within the EU and EEA. The EU public procurement rules extend to those countries in Central and Eastern Europe that have concluded Europe agreements with the EU. They also have to consider the effects of the World Trade Organization Agreement on General Procurement which came into effect in a significant number of countries in 1996 and which has different thresholds, but is otherwise similar to the EU rules. These mean that they will not only have to contend with their national and European rivals in bidding for contracts, but also with competitors from for example the USA, Japan and Korea. On the plus side, they should be looking to bid for contracts in those countries too.

The greatest difficulty is keeping an eye open for opportunities, and besides scanning the *Official Journal*, consulting TED, and getting information from European Information Offices, it may be useful to keep in touch with UK Rep, the EIB and even local embassies and Commission representations in the various countries.

It would also be wise to access the Market Access Database on the Internet on http://mkaccdb.eu.int (free of charge to EU users), to find out what sort of trade barriers you might encounter, rates of duty, etc. It also has a useful guide to import formalities.

It should here be noted that there are lucrative contracts available under the Community banner in many developing countries (see Part VII on the Lomé Convention).

As may be expected, tendering for a contract may be expensive, and difficult if you are a SME, but there is help available, as there is a political drive evidenced in the Agenda 2000 document for example, to make the EU as a whole competitive. This necessitates helping small firms too. Thus in many of the Community's own programmes there is specific provision for SMEs, and help for them generally in finding partners and obtaining finance. The Department of Trade and Industry is a useful starting point, or local Chambers of Commerce, trade or professional organizations, all of whom should have useful advice; and TED.

Finally, particularly with regard to consultancy opportunities, there is no substitute for direct contact with the Commission, as consultants who wish to apply for contract work with regard to the various studies and analyses commissioned particularly for ACP contracts under the Lomé Convention have to be registered with the Commission before they can be considered. As often little or no publicity is given with regard to consultancy work, there is no substitute in this area for regular contact by telephone, fax or letter, if not in person.

Part VII

International matters

THE EXPANDING EUROPEAN UNION

Mention has already been made of the 11 states that have applied to join the EU. Much has been written, and studies have been undertaken, and projects put in hand. There are programmes targeted at helping the applicant states to achieve the economic and attitudinal development, together with, for many, the achievement of an understanding and ability to work in a free market necessary to enable them to survive in the greater competitive environment of the EU.

The peaceful revolution which swept Eastern Europe in 1989 was probably the most significant event, in global terms, of the past 45 years. It happened on the very doorstep of the EC, and represented both a challenge, and an opportunity for the EC. The new members would be joining a very different Community to that set up by the Rome Treaty. At a very practical level, the new enlargement will increase the number of languages from the present 11, to a possible 15, and so further complicate the work of the Community. The applicant countries are trying to operate in a new market-oriented way, and many still have almost insuperable economic and cultural difficulties. The series of cooperation and trade agreements with many are helping. Association and Europe agreements have been concluded with all the applicant states. The European Bank for Reconstruction and Development (EBRD) was set up in April 1991 to provide loans and credits to Eastern Europe The programmes, too, have been working, and the most well known of these is the PHARE programme, the aim of which was to help originally Hungary and Poland, but has now been extended to other Eastern European and Baltic States, to build a democratic, free enterprise market economy able to compete effectively in the Single Market. TACIS was similar to PHARE, and aimed originally at the Newly Independent States (NIS) and Mongolia. Under PHARE significant financial assistance from G24 is coordinated by the Commission.

The Central and East European States that have applied for full membership of the EU have done so because they regard this as the basis for their political development and stability in the future. Each of the Association agreements signed by the EC with the CEES sets out the general conditions for full membership of the EU. Six major conditions have to be met:

1. the capacity of the country concerned to assume the obligations of membership (known collectively as the '*acquis communautaire*')
2. the stability of institutions in the candidate country guaranteeing democracy, law, human rights and respect for ethnic minorities
3. the existence of a market economy
4. the candidate country's endorsement of the EU's objectives as regards economic and monetary union
5. the ability of the country to cope with the competitive rigours of Community membership
6. the Community's ability to absorb new members and at the same time ensure that the momentum of European integration is not adversely affected.

Agenda 2000 is a policy for a stronger and wider Union produced in 1997 by the Commission, and endorsed by the Council, that looked at the challenges facing the EU in the new millennium, and focused on the need to consolidate existing policies and to look at what was needed in the context of enlargement, primarily further institutional reform and a review of the Commission's organization and operations; developing internal policies for growth, employment and quality of life, including creating the conditions for sustainable growth and employment, and encouraging the Information Society; further reform of the Common Agricultural Policy; and the setting up of a new financial framework for 2000–2006 to take into account the costs and economic impact of absorbing new Member States.

The IGC which concluded with the Amsterdam Treaty had been scheduled to deal with the institutional and decision-making needs of the existing EU to take account of the future needs of an enlarged Community. Since then, the European Conference on EU enlargement has taken place in March 1998 when the leaders of the 26 countries (EU 15 plus 11 applicants) came together to discuss the different aspects such as competitiveness, agricultural and environmental issues, regional cooperation, cross-border crime and foreign and security policy. Also in March 1998

Accession Partnership (AP) Agreements were signed with 10 Eastern European applicant states (Bulgaria, Czech Republic, Estonia, Hungary, Latvia, Lithuania, Poland, Romania, Slovakia and Slovenia) as part of the preparations for them to join the EU. These APs concentrate on the 6 membership criteria which were agreed at the Copenhagen Council in 1993 and provide for advice and financial assistance. Accession negotiations have now formally opened with six applicants: Cyprus, Czech Republic, Estonia, Hungary, Poland and Slovenia.

In the June 1998 EU summit, more progress was made, in that March 1999 was set as a deadline for agreeing the various measures necessary in the context of enlargement, such as CAP reform and a seven-year budget deal to take into account regional aid necessary up until 2006. This despite the warning shots sent concerning the reluctance of some of the larger states to increase their contributions to the EU budget.

It is undoubtedly true that enlargement of the kind envisaged will put the EU under considerable strain, but account should be taken of the long-term benefits achievable, and the great strides forward that some applicants have achieved in a very short time.

EXTERNAL RELATIONS, POLICIES AND TRADE

The importance of the Community relations with other countries has been growing in importance as its economic clout has grown until now it accounts for over one-fifth of world trade. Originally a common commercial policy was seen as important as regards the relationship of the EC with third countries, and this led to various common customs tariffs and then to trade and cooperation agreements with third countries. Increasingly, international trade negotiations have been concluded at Community level, eg with the World Trade Organization (WTO).

Much could be written concerning trade relations with countries outside the EU. These range from the close associations, akin to membership of the Community without the right to participate in legislative procedures of the non-EU countries of the EEA (Iceland, Liechtenstein and Norway), to Europe agreements with the applicant countries, to general cooperation agreements with other countries. Relations with the ACP developing countries is explained separately (see page 116.) and it is interesting to note that EC and ASEAN (Association of South East Asian Nations) foreign ministers have been meeting regularly since 1978. There are many programmes of assistance, and the EU has a special responsibility concerning economic assistance, development cooperation and humanitarian aid with many countries.

To give just some examples. There are close trading links with many countries such as the USA with whom there seem to be a raft of trade disputes on a variety of issues, albeit deeper relations are now developing. Thus a 1998 US/EU anti-trust agreement was signed in June which is in effect a competition policy accord to deal with and avoid access to market disputes, by enabling US and EU competition officials to cooperate in both investigation and enforcement of anti-trust complaints. Trade relations with Japan are also developing consistently and there are now regular meetings between MEPs and members of the Japanese Diet. The Community's trade agreements with the Mediterranean countries date back to the 1970, and have been regularly updated since, with various aid and trade provisions. Relations with Central and Eastern European countries are developing fast as the pre-accession and accession negotiations continue with many of them and the PHARE programme provides valuable assistance. Russia and the Ukraine are useful trading partners, and there are various partnership and cooperation agreements with many countries in the former USSR. Relations with China are changing fast, as Hong Kong was the EU's tenth largest trading partner, and an annual summit between China and the EU is likely in the future. Recent events have shown just how inter-dependent are the economies of East and West.

COMMON FOREIGN AND SECURITY POLICY (CFSP)

The arrangements for negotiating trade policy have been rather different from that regulating general foreign and security policies *vis-à-vis* third countries. Thus, in the 1970s the procedures for coordinating the national foreign policies of the Member States were achieved through European Political Cooperation (EPC). However, there were difficulties in achieving consensus that inhibited the swift cohesive decisions by Member States frequently needed in reacting to international scenarios. This led to the establishment of Foreign and Security Policy as a separate pillar of the EU under the TEU which came into force in November 1993. Under this, CFSP remained within the sphere of national sovereignty, and was to be organized through inter-governmental cooperation. The objectives of CFSP were set out in Article J.1(2) of the TEU and were:

- to safeguard the common values, fundamental interests and independence of the EU
- to strengthen the security of the EU and its Member States
- to preserve peace and strengthen international security
- to promote international cooperation
- to develop and consolidate democracy and the rule of law, and respect for human rights and fundamental freedoms.

Under Article J.1(4) the Member States agreed to support these principles and to refrain from any action which is contrary to the interests of the EU or likely to impair its effectiveness as a cohesive force in international relations.

Although NATO is central to the EU's defence, yet the Western European Union (WEU) is being developed as a key element of the development of a EU defence policy, it being noted that ten of the EU's Member States are also members of the WEU, with the emphasis being on peacekeeping and participation in humanitarian operations.

The Amsterdam Treaty, which is now close to ratification, enables the EU to act more coherently in external relations as it provides for agreement by consensus for common strategies for joint action, and on the basis of majority voting on the actions themselves, with certain safeguards for Member States who do not wish to participate.

There are inevitably difficulties which will test the resolve of the Foreign Ministers with regard to common action, but a clearer European identity in security and defence matters does seem to be emerging.

Further information on this area of EU policy can be obtained from the Commission UK Representation which has useful booklets available, from the EIOs or the Internet: Europa server (http:/ /europa.eu.int) or from the Foreign and Commonwealth Office.

THE DEVELOPING WORLD

Although the nations of the EU have their own aid programmes, and the EU does not attempt to interfere with these, yet the TEU in 1992 contained a new section on development cooperation and included specific objectives for the EU to support the development of the various countries concerned. This resulted from a perceived need to achieve increased coordination between the aid and development policies, in particular, trade and agriculture, of the Member States and the Community with regard to this growing area.

Community help for developing countries in the African, Caribbean and Pacific Regions (ACP countries) are primarily governed by the Lomé Conventions. In fact, the scope of Lomé is now very wide, taking in some 70 countries, and there are cooperation agreements with some southern and eastern Mediterranean states as well as some countries in Asia and Latin America.

Lomé IV runs until 2000, and the mid-term review has resulted in a strengthening of some of the objectives, such as the defence of human rights, and to increase democracy, and there are provisions to suspend cooperation with ACP states because of civil war or human rights violations. It also gave greater priority to developing ACP trade to encourage competitiveness and the gradual integration of those countries into the world economy. Preferences are used as a means of developing trade, and are given with regard to a wide variety of goods with limited exceptions, and some tariff quotas also apply; but there are also other trade development programmes. The STABEX system was set up in the 1970 to help ACP states to achieve stability by guaranteeing earnings on certain products. The funds available under Lomé are large – ECU12.5 billion in the years 1991–95 and ECU14.625 billion for the period 1996–2000 – and are administered by the European Development Fund (EDF) that offers grants or loans at particularly low rates of interest. The nations concerned submit outline programmes to the Commission for spending the funds they are given or loaned, and suggest specific projects within this framework. Following agreement, tenders are put out, and may be allotted, preference being given to local Lomé Convention country firms. However, there are many lucrative contracts to be gained, payments for which are made directly through the EDF, and so are effectively risk-free.

The funds support three main areas:

- agriculture
- transport infrastructure and energy
- mining.

Three kinds of contracts are financed:

- works contracts (eg roads, drainage and irrigation schemes, etc)
- supply contracts (eg agricultural plant and equipment, fertilizer, etc)
- service contracts (eg training programmes and feasibility studies).

It should be noted that there are also other funds available to these countries under separate programmes such as for the protection of tropical forests, or combating AIDS.

As to how to tender: advice may be obtained from the Department of Trade and Industry, from the European Commission DG for Development Information Unit in Brussels (telephone: 32 (2) 299 30 62) or from your local European Information Office. Tender Electronics Daily (TED) gives details of calls for tenders.

Part VIII

How to contact the EU institutions to lobby or for information

There is a widely held belief that the European Commission is overstaffed. This is not so. For many Community affairs there are only one or two officials directly concerned with specific matters, and it is always possible that they will not have English as their main language. It must be said, however, that this is not usually a problem, but you may find it easier to write to or fax the Commission with your problem, directing your communication to the appropriate Directorate-General. Telephoning Brussels is more expensive, but it may be the quickest and easiest way to get through to the person you need to contact, and there is policy of openness in the Commission.

If you are intending to lobby in Brussels or Strasbourg, it is vital that you have a well-researched, properly prepared brief. The government departments in this country have useful information, and the Department of Trade is a useful starting place, although the subject matter will determine the department you should consult and liaise with. They will have useful links with their opposite numbers in the Commission.

The Information Offices and Representation of the European Commission in London are very helpful, as is the London office of the European Parliament. Lists of where to obtain information are given at the end of this book, but do not forget the Commission website on the Internet: (http://www.cec.org.uk).

It is useful to know that the *Official Journal of the European Communities* which is published daily sets out an impressive amount of information which is divided into three different series:

1. The L series publishes the full text of all adopted legislation within a short time of full adoption.

2. The C series sets out the full text of all formal draft legislation – ie when it has been submitted by the Commission to the Council of Ministers, and after Council amendments. It also includes other matters, such as calls to submit proposals under EU funding programmes.
3. The S series provides details of works, service and supplies contracts above a prescribed value issued in Member States.

It is, however, time-consuming to keep abreast of published information, so you may also need to contact other bodies – the British Standards Institution (BSI) are heavily involved in discussions about new standards, and often have difficulty in getting feedback from the enterprises which will be affected by new standards.

It is useful to remember that the European Parliament is an important force in the legislative process, so your local MEP could be most helpful, especially if he or she is on the appropriate EP Committee. If not, then you should consider putting your matter before the appropriate Committee of the EP. If it is a problem relating to maladministration of a Commission Department, for example, you could contact the Ombudsman of the EP. MPs at Westminster have useful links with their counterparts at the EP, and as your problem would be a matter of Community importance (as probably otherwise you would not be seeking to lobby in the EU institutions) it is always wise to have your national MP and Government Departments on your side. You could also contact the ECOSOC as their members are both knowledgeable and influential.

The Committee of the Regions is another body with national representatives, and it, too, is influential in the matters on which it has to be consulted – such as regional policies, TENs, cultural policies or public health, and other matters on which the Commission thinks they should be consulted, so it could be useful to contact your local representative.

Possibly the most useful place to start in terms of seeking out the best person to deal with in the Commission is UK Rep, the UK Representation in Brussels, who generally know exactly what is going on where. On no account visit Brussels on Community matters without contacting the UK Rep staff who necessarily have a wide knowledge of what is going on. They can help greatly to ease your difficulties, and avoid wasting your time and that of others. Their address, together with other useful addresses, is listed at the back of this book.

It should be remembered that there is a Code of Conduct for lobbyists (written on the basis that there is no such thing as a free lunch) and it may be that you should obtain the services of a professional lobbyist if the

matter is serious, as he or she will be fully cognisant of the various procedures, the proper committees to write to, and the individuals with particular
interests who might be more likely to take your matter on board. Beware,
however, the expensive hangers-on. Try to use personal recommendations
when choosing your lobbyist or expert to help.

Make sure that you are lobbying wherever you can, and timing is important, as is appropriate press support or coverage. Finally, it is always useful
to have a good knowledge of the procedure which will be followed with
regard to the matter which concerns you. It may move more quickly (or
indeed more slowly) than you expect.

EURO-INFORMATION AVAILABILITY

A problem which affects all enterprises, large and small, is the vast volume
and sheer complexity of information available which could be of real use to
them – and might indeed be vital to the success of their business. You have
to know about a project before you can tender for it. There are significant
costs in tendering, and it may be important to choose the right partners
quickly. To address these problems the Commission has instituted a website. Thus a great deal of information on the EU itself, and most of its publications are available on the Internet through Europaserver
(http//europa.eu.int). In addition to this, there are many individual databases, over 50 online and CD-ROM databases, Internet-based services and
document delivery services produced by the European Commission, European Parliament, and other Community institutions are listed in a very useful publication produced by the Commission: *'The European Union
Database Directory'* produced by the Office for Official Publications of the
European Communities.

For example TED (Tender Electronics Daily) was set up to facilitate
searches for suitable projects, and is an on-line directory of invitations to
tender for public works and supply contracts, and its information is available from the European Information Centres. The BRITE (Basic Research
in Industrial Technologies for Europe) scheme was specifically amended to
facilitate involvement by small and medium-sized enterprises (SMEs).
Some Framework Programmes specifically reserve a proportion of their
budgets to tenders by SME, and the Fifth Framework Research and
Development Programme for 1998–2002 targets the encouragement of
technological exploitation and provides safeguards for SMEs both in terms

of finance, and information and training, quality enhancement and partner and business search networks, for example through BRE and Business Co-operation Network (BC-Net). The latter was set up in 1988 specifically to encourage an awareness of increasing business opportunities in Europe, and is aimed at giving enterprises a framework within which to expand, and the practical means through specialist support to develop commercial, financial and technical co-operation at a European level.

Because the information deficit tends particularly to affect SMEs, the Commission has a telephone helpline for SMEs (010 32 22 36 5151).

The general public may have different needs, and the Commission has just set up 'Europe Direct' which has a Freephone number in the UK for general information about the EU on 0800 581 591, and an Internet website on (http://europa.eu.int/citizens).

The sheer volume of information about Europe, the EU, integration, policies, legislation, and every other possible aspect is daunting, and much depends on which aspect you wish to explore.

Some advice, however: old news is no news, and old law is bad law. What I mean by this is that situations, attitudes and proposals shift ground quite quickly in the European scene, and to quote another old adage: a week is a long time in politics – so beware of old books and studies. Much may be seen in quite a different light when it is written about only a few weeks later. If you can keep up to date with what is going on, you will find a fascinating progression.

If you have access to the Internet, then a wealth of information is available to you, and a list of useful Internet numbers is given in Appendix II on page 127. You can get information from the European Commission itself in Brussels (see 'Useful Addresses') or from the UK Press and Information Offices of the European Commission.

Catalogue of Publications was produced in May 1998 by the Representation in the UK of the European Commission of publications available (for single units at least) free of charge in the UK. This includes useful material for schools as well as general and specific policy documents. The various Euro-Information Centres (EICs) are listed in Appendix V.

If you have a professional or trade organization, or belong to a Trade Union or Chamber of Commerce, then they should have the right contacts who have just the information you need which might save you many hours of research. The Statistical Office of the European Communities has useful information and reports, both written and on-line, and a list of useful sources of additional information is included in Appendix V.

A last word of warning: the situation and the provisions can change with great rapidity, so do try to get up-to-the-minute information. If, however, you know the background, you will be better able to ask all the right questions.

Good hunting!

Appendix I

European Commissioners and their portfolios

President Jacques SANTER
Luxembourgish
Secretariat-General
Legal Service
Security Office
Forward Studies Unit
Inspectorate-General
Joint Interpreting and Conference Service (JICS)
Spokesman's Service
Monetary matters (with Mr de Silguy)
Common foreign and security policy and human
    rights (with Mr Van den Broek)
Institutional questions and Intergovernmental
    Conference (with Mr Oreja)

Karel VAN MIERT
Belgian
Competition

Marcelino OREJA
Spanish
Relations with the European Parliament
Relations with the Member States (transparency,
    communication and information)
Culture and audiovisual policy
Office for Official Publications Institutional
    matters and preparations for the 1996
Intergovernmental Conference (in agreement
    with the President)

Monika WULF-MATHIES
German
Regional policies
Relations with the Committee of the Regions
Cohesion Fund (in agreement with Mr Kinnock
    and Mrs Bjerregaard)

Emma BONINO
Italian
Fisheries
Consumer policy
European Community
Humanitarian Office (ECHO)

Vice-President Sir Leon BRITTAN
British
External relations with North America,
    Australia, New Zealand, Japan, China, Korea,
    Hong Kong, Macao and Taiwan
Common commercial policy
Relations with the OECD and WTO

Hans VAN DEN BROEK
Dutch
External relations with the countries of Central
    and Eastern Europe (CEECs), the former
    Soviet Union, Mongolia, Turkey, Cyprus,
    Malta and other European countries
Common foreign and security policy (CFSP)
    and human rights (in agreement with the
    President)
External missions

Anita GRADIN
Swedish
Immigration, home affairs and justice
Relations with the Ombudsman
Financial control
Fraud prevention

Neil KINNOCK
British
Transport (including trans-European
    networks)

Yves-Thibault de SILGUY
French
Economic and financial affairs
Monetary matters
(in agreement with the President)
Credit and investments
Statistical Office

Vice-President Manuel MARÍN
Spanish
External relations with southern Mediterranean
  countries, the Middle East, Latin America
  and Asia (except Japan, China, Korea, Hong
  Kong, Macao and Taiwan) including
  development aid

João de Deus PINHEIRO
Portuguese
External relations with African, Caribbean and
  Pacific countries (ACP) and South Africa,
  including development aid
Lomé Convention

Édith CRESSON
French
Science, research and development
Joint Research Centre
Human resources, education, training and youth

Mario MONTI
Italian
Internal market
Financial services and financial integration
Customs
Taxation

Erkki LIIKANEN
Finnish
Budget
Personnel and administration
Translation and in-house computer services

Martin BANGEMANN
German
Industrial affairs
Information and telecommunications
  technologies

Pádraig FLYNN
Irish
Employment and social affairs
Relations with the Economic and Social
  Committee

Ritt BJERREGAARD
Danish
Environment
Nuclear safety

Franz FISCHLER
Austrian
Agriculture and rural development

Christos PAPOUTSIS
Greek
Energy and Euratom Supply Agency
Small business
Tourism

Source: European Commission 1995–2000, published by DG$\overline{\text{X}}$, The European Commission, Brussels.

Appendix II

Finding Europe on the Internet

The Commission has produced a directory of electronic databases, but some useful web sites are set out below.

Council of the European Union
http://agenor.consilium.eu.int

European Parliament
http://www.europarl.eu.int
Parliament agendas, press releases and other information. UK Representation Office
http://www.cec.org.uk/ep/index.htm

European Ombudsman
http://www.euro-ombudsman.eu.int

European Commission
http://europa.eu.int
General useful information, and daily official information service and links to other EU and government servers
UK Representation Office
http://www.cec.org.uk
Press information (RAPID)
http://europa.eu.int/en/comm/spp/rapid.html
Who's who in the EU (IDEA)
http://europa.eu.int/ideaen.html

European Court of Justice
http://europa.eu.int/cj/

Court of Auditors
http://www.eca.eu.int

Committee of the Regions
http://europa.eu/int/comreg/comreg.html

Economic and Social Committee
http://europa.eu.int/ces/ces.html

European Centre for the Development of Vocational Training
http://www.cedefop.gr

European Environment Agency
http://www.eea.dk

**European Foundation for the Improvement
of Living and Working Conditions**
http://europa.eu.int/agencies/efilwc/

European Medicinal Evaluation Agency
http://www.eudra.org/emea.html

European Investment Bank
http://www.eib.org

European Monetary Institute
http://europa.eu.int/emi/emi.html

European Training Foundation
http://www.etf.it

**Office for Harmonization in
the Internal Market**
http://europa.eu.int/agencies/ohim/ohim.htm

INFORMATION FOR RESEARCHERS, ACADEMICS AND STUDENTS

Some web addresses are given in the text of this book, but a further list is here.

Ecsa-Net
http://europa.eu.int/ecsa/homepage.html
This interactive network seeks to encourage collaboration between European integration
studies academies teaching

Eurodicautom
http://www2.echo.lu/edic/
Multilingual technological database

Eurolib-Per
http://www2.echo.lu/echo/databases/eurolib/en/e193-hom.html
This is a useful catalogue of periodicals in the libraries of the EU institutions

Eur-Op's Homepage
http://www.europa.eu.int/en/comm/opoce/wel.html
Provides information on the EU's publishing house

Eurostat
http://europa.eu.int/en/comm/eurostat/eurostat.html
(European Statistical Office Information)

Information concerning student grants and loans
http://www.oprn.gov.uk/dfee/dfeehme.hton
Postgraduate awards are also available and information as to these has been produced
by the European Commission, Representation in the UK background report entitled
'European Educational Integration and Student Grants'

Joint Research Centres
http://www.jrc.org

Ortelius
http://ortelius.unifi.it
This provides data on universities, colleges, academics and apprenticeship possibilities in
Europe; annual subscription required

Appendix III

The European Commission: contacting the departments

A full and detailed list of the various departments of the Commission and the names of the people who are responsible for them can be found in Vacher's European Companion, and in the European Community's own publication *Who's Who in the European Union? An Inter Institutional Directory*. For convenience, the main titles of departments are listed below to give an idea of the breadth of work of the Commission, and to enable readers to find appropriate Directorates and departments to contact for particular subjects. The postal address of the Commission is:

The European Commission
Rue de la Loi 200
B-1049
Brussels
Belgium
Tel: 00 32 2 229 11 11
Web site: *http://europa.eu.net*

In the list set out below, postal addresses have been indicated only where they differ from the main address above.
If, however only general information is needed, then it may be easier to write to or contact the European Commission in the UK. Their addresses are:

**The European Commission
Representation in the United Kingdom**
8 Storey's Gate, London SW1P 3AT
0171 973 1992 Fax 0171 973 1900

**The European Commission
Representation in Northern Ireland**
Windsor House, 9/15 Bedford Street,
Belfast BT2 7EG
01232 240708 Fax 01232 248241

**The European Commission
Representation in Scotland**
9 Alva Street, Edinburgh EH2 4PH
0131 225 2058 Fax 0131 226 4105

**The European Commission
Representative in Wales**
4 Cathedral Road,
Cardiff CF1 9SG

As there have been widespread renovations to the Commission's old headquarters in Brussels, staff have been relocated, so it is wise to check exactly where appointments with officials will be held.

The Different Departments and Directorates General of the European Commission

Secretariat-General of the Commission
Rue de la Loi 200, 1049 Brussels, Belgium
00 32 2 299 11 11
Fax 00 32 2 295 0122/23/24

Administrative Unit

Directorate A Registry

Directorate B
Coordination I
Institutional matters, Community law,
information technology and publications
and documentary databases

Directorate C
Coordination II
Internal coordination and planning;
organisation of departments; and grants

Directorate D
Relations with the Council

Directorate E
Relations with the European Parliament,
the European Ombudsman, the Economic
and Social Committee, the Committee of
the Regions and trade and industry

Directorate F
Coordination of fraud prevention

TITLE VI TEU TASK FORCE (cooperation on justice and home affairs)

FORWARD STUDIES UNIT
(under the direct authority of the President)

Inspectorate-General

Legal Service

Spokesman's Service

**Joint Interpretation and Conference
Service**

Administrative Unit

Directorate A
Interpretation, Training, Documentation

Directorate B
Interpretation and Conferences

Statistical Office (EUROSTAT)

Units responsible for the integrated
management of resources   reporting
directly to the Director-General

Directorate A
Statistical information system; research
and data analysis; technical cooperation
with Phare and Tacis countries

Directorate B
Economic statistics and economic and
monetary convergence

Directorate C
Information and dissemination; transports;
technical cooperation with non-member
countries (except Phare and Tacis
countries); external and intra-Community
trade statistics

Directorate D
Business statistics

Directorate E
Social and regional statistics and
geographical information system

Directorate F
Agricultural, environmental and energy
statistics

Translation Service

Directorate for General and Language
Matters

Directorate for Translation – Brussels

B Economic and financial affairs, internal
market and competition

C Agriculture, fisheries, regional policies
and structural policies

D External relations, customs union,
development, enlargement and
humanitarian   aid

E Research, telecommunications, energy
industry, environment and transport

Directorate for Translation – Luxembourg

F Social affairs, human resources and
consumer policy

G Statistics, enterprise policy, information market and innovation

Informatics Directorate

Security Office

Directorates General of the Commission

Directorate General

External Relations: Commercial Policy and Relations with North America, the Far East, Australia and New Zealand

Directorate B
Relations with North America, Australia, New Zealand, NAFTA and APEC

Directorate C
Antidumping strategy; dumping aspects (policy, investigations and measures)

Directorate D
Sectoral commercial questions

Directorate E
Antidumping strategy; injury and Community interest aspects (policy, investigations and measures); other instruments of external economic policy and general questions
Directorate F
Relations with Far Eastern countries

Directorate G
WTO, OECD, commercial questions with respect to agriculture and fisheries, export credit policy

Directorate M
Services, investments, TRIMS, dual use goods, standards and certification, external relations in the research, science, nuclear energy and environment fields

External Delegations to International Organizations

Directorate-General IA
External Relations: Europe and New Independent States, Common Foreign and Security Policy, and External Missions

Directorate A
Multilateral relations

Directorate B
Relations with Central European Countries

Directorate C
Relations with the New Independent States (NIS) and Mongolia

Directorate D
Relations with Other European Countries

Directorate E
Management of External Missions

Directorate F
Direction of human and financial resources and coordination

Directorate-General IB
External Relations: Southern Mediterranean, Middle East, Latin America, South and South-East Asia and North-South Co-operation

Directorate A
Southern Mediterranean and Middle and Near East

Directorate B
Latin America

Directorate C
South and South-East Asia

Directorate D
North-South relations

Directorate E
Finance and resources

Directorate-General II
Economic and Financial Affairs
Administrative Unit

Directorate A
National economies

Directorate B
Economic service

Directorate C
Surveillance of the Community economy

Directorate D
Monetary matters

Directorate E
Financial instruments and capital
movements

Directorate F
International economic and financial
matters

Financial Operations Service (FOS)

Directorate FOS – A: Financial
Engineering

Directorate FOS – B: ECSC Activities

Directorate-General III

Industry

Administrative Unit
Integrated resources management

Directorate A
Industrial policy

Directorate B
Legislation and standardization; telematics
networks

Directorate C
Industrial Affairs I; Basic industries

Directorate D
Industrial Affairs II: Capital goods
industries

Directorate E
Industrial Affairs III: Consumer goods
industries

Directorate F
R & TD: Information technologies

Directorate-General IV
Competition

Directorate A
Competition policy, Co-ordination,
International Affairs and Relations with
other Institutions

Directorate B
Merger Task Force

Directorate C
Information, communication and multimedia

Directorate D
Services

Directorate E
Basic industries and Energy

Directorate F
Capital and consumer goods industries

Directorate G
State aids

Directorate-General V
Employment, Industrial Relations and
Social Affairs

Administrative Unit
Reporting direct to the Director-General

Directorate A
Employment and Labour Market

Directorate B
European Social Fund: policy development

Directorate C
European Social Fund: Operation

Directorate D
Social Dialogue, social and equal rights

Directorate E
Social policy and action

Directorate F
Public Health and Safety at work

Directorate G
Management of resources

Directorate-General VI
Agriculture

Directorate A
Economic analyses, forward studies

Directorate A1
Administration and general matters,
budgetary and financial relations; clearance
of EAGGF accounts; evaluation

Directorate A2
Relations with the European Parliament
and other Institutions; Information and
Informatics

Directorate B1
Agro-economic legislation

Directorate BII
Public, Animal and Plant health

Directorate C
Organization of markets in crop products

Directorate D
Organization of markets in livestock
products

Directorate E
Organization of markets in specialised
crops

Directorate F1
Rural development I

Directorate FII
Rural Development II

Directorate G
Agricultural budgetary and financial
matters

Directorate H
International affairs relating to
Agriculture

Directorate-General VII
Transport

Directorate A
International relations and transeuropean
transport network and infrastructures

Directorate B
Inland transport

Directorate C
Air transport

Directorate D
Maritime transport

Directorate E
Development of transport policy and
research and development

Directorate-General VIII
Development

Administrative Units
Directly attached to the Director-General,
Administrative Board of the European
Association for Co-operation (EAC)

Directorate A
Development policy

Directorate B
Instruments

Directorate C
Management of financial and human
resources

Directorate D
West and Central Africa

Directorate E
Eastern and Southern Africa

Directorate F
Caribbean, Pacific, Indian Ocean

Directorate G
Sectoral Implementation

Directorate General IX
Personnel and Administration

Administrative Unit
Reporting direct to the Director-General

Reporting direct to the Deputy Director-
General (Luxembourg)

Directorate A
Personnel

Directorate B
Rights and obligations

Directorate C
Administration

Directorate-General X
Information, Communication, Culture,
Audiovisual

Directorate A
Central Information Office

Directorate B
Information Networks

Directorate C
Audiovisual policy, culture and sport

Directorate D
Communication

Directorate General XI
Environment, Nuclear Safety and Civil
Protection

Directorate A
General and international affairs

Directorate B
Environmental instruments

Directorate C
Nuclear safety and civil protection

Directorate D
Environment quality and natural resources

Directorate E
Industry and environment

Directorate-General XII
Science, Research and Development

Directorate AG
General Administrative Affairs

Directorate AS
RDT: Strategy and Coordination

Directorate AP
RDT: Framework Programme

Directorate B
RTD: Cooperation with Non-Member
Countries and International Organizations

Directorate C
RTD: Industrial and Materials
Technologies

Directorate D
RTD: Environment

Directorate E
RTD: Life Sciences and Technologies

Directorate F
RTD: Energies

Directorate G
RTD: Human Capital and Mobility,
Targeted socio-economic research

Joint Research Centre
Programmes Directorate (Brussels)

Coordination of Resources – ISPRA
1–21020 Ispra, Italy
00 39 332 78 91 11
Fax 00 39 332 78 90 45

Institute for Reference Materials and
Measurements – GEEL
Steenweg op Retie, B–2440 Geel, Belgium
00 32 2 14 571 211
Fax 00 32 2 14 584 273

Institute for Transuranium Elements –
KARLSRUHE
Linkenheim Postfach 2340, D–76125,
Karlsruhe, Germany
00 49 721 47 9510
Fax 00 49 72 47 951 590

Institute for Advanced Materials –
PETTEN AND ISPRA
Westerdvinweg 3, Postbus Nr2
175 SZG-Petten, NH, The Netherlands
00 31 22 456 56 56
Fax 00 31 22 56 33 93

Institute for Systems Informatics and
Safety – ISPRA
Fax 00 39 332 78 99 23

Environment Institute ISPRA
Fax 00 39 332 78 92 22

Institute for Space Applications ISPRA
Fax 00 39 332 78 95 36

Institute for Prospective Technological
Studies Seville
World Trade Centre
Isla de la Cartuja, s/n, E–41092
Seville, Spain
00 34 5448 8273
Fax 00 34 5448 8274

Directorate-General XIII
Telecommunications, Information Market
and Exploitation of Research

Information Society Project Office (ISPO)

International aspects of information society
and telecommunications

Units reporting direct to the Director-
General

Directorate A
Telecommunications, trans-European
networks and services, and postal services

Directorate B
Advanced communications technologies
and services

Directorate C
Telematics applications (networks and
services)

Directorate D
Dissemination and exploitation of R & TD
results, technology transfer and
innovation
Directorate E
Information industry and market and
language processing

Directorate-General XIV
Fisheries

Directorate A
Horizontal measures and markets

Directorate B
International fisheries organizations and
fisheries agreements

Directorate C
Conservation policy and monitoring

Directorate D
Structures and areas dependent on fisheries

Directorate-General XV
Internal Market and Financial Services

Directorate A
General matters and coordination; Free
movements of persons and direct taxation

Directorate B
Free movement of goods and public
procurement

Directorate C
Financial Institutions

Directorate D
Free movement of information; company
law and financial information

Directorate E
Intellectual and industrial property freedom
of establishment and freedom to   provide
services, notably in the regulated
professions and the media

Directorate General XVI
Regional Policy and Cohesion

Directorate A
Formulation of regional policies

Directorate B
Regional assistance in Belgium, Denmark,
Luxembourg, the Netherlands, Greece,
Portugal, Austria, Finland and Sweden

Directorate C
Regional Assistance in Spain, Ireland,
Northern Ireland and Italy

Directorate D
Regional Assistance in Germany, France
and the United Kingdom

Directorate E
Cohesion Fund

Directorate F
Budgetry and financial management,
communication and computer services

Directorate G
Coordination and evaluation of operations

Directorate-General XVII
Energy

Directorate A – Energy policy

Directorate B – Industries and markets of
Fossil fuels

Directorate C
Industries and Markets of Non-fossil Fuels

Directorate D
Energy Technology

Luxembourg
Directorate E
Euratom Safeguards

Directorate-General XVIII
Now a service of DG II. See DG II
Financial Operations Service

Directorate-General XIX
Budgets
Administrative Unit

Directorate A
Expenditure

Directorate B
Resources

Directorate C
Budget Implementation

Directorat-General XX
Financial Control

Directorate A
Control of administrative expenditure,
internal policies; accounting and Sincom

Directorate B
Control of flanking policies (ERDF, ESF,
EAGGF Guidance Section), Cohesion
Fund, IMPs, borrowing and lending
operations

Directorate C
Control of revenue; control of EAGGF
Guarantee Section; control of external
action expenditure

Directorate-General XXI
Customs and Indirect Taxation
Administration Unit

Directorate A
General matters

Directorate B
Customs

Directorate C
Indirect taxation

Directorate-General XXII
Education, Training and Youth

Directorate A
Actions in the field of education,
Implementation of the SOCRATES
programme

Directorate B
Vocational training policy

Directorate C
Cooperation with non-member countries,
actions in the field of youth, publications
and information

Directorate-General XXIII
Enterprise Policy, Distributive Trades,
Tourism and Cooperatives

Directorate A
Community strategy for enterprise
development and improvement of the
business environment

Directorate B
Information for businesses, business
cooperation and strengthening
competitiveness

Directorate C
Concerted action under enterprise and
tourism policy

Directorate-General XXIV
Consumer Policy and Health Protection

Directorate A
Community actions in consumers' interest

Directorate B
Scientific opinions on health

Directorate C
Co-ordination of horizontal matters

Food and Veterinary Office (FVO)
(Ireland)
Trident House, Rockhill Main Street,
Blackrock, Co. Dublin, Ireland

**European Community Humanitarian
Office (ECHO)**
Rue de la Loi 200, B–1049, Brussels,
Belgium
00 32 2 299 11 11
Fax 00 32 2 295 45 78

Euratom Supply Agency
Address as above
Fax 00 32 2 295 05 27

**EUR-OP (Office for Official
Publications of the European
Communities)**

2 rue mercier, L–2985 Luxembourg
00 352 29 291
Fax 00 352 495 719

Appendix IV

Sources of additional information

Reproduced from the fifth edition of *The EC/EU Fact Book*, by Alex Roney, published by Kogan Page.

This Appendix gives various sources of extra information and advice referred to in the text. It should be noted that the Commission has made various databases available to the public, some of which are listed in Appendix II. These include ELEX, which covers all community legislation; and INFO 1992, which gives information on the transposition of measures made in the context of the completion of the Single Market. The UK Representation of the European Commission site on the World Wide Web is: http://www.cec.org.uk.

Anti-Counterfeiting Group
PO Box 578
High Wycombe
Buckinghamshire HP13 5FY
Tel: 01494 449165

Anti-fraud Hotline in the UK
Freephone 0800 963 595

Association Européenne des Industries de Produits de Marque (AIM)
Rue de l'Orme 19
B-1040, Brussels
Belgium

Bank of England
Threadneedle Street
London EC2R 8AH
Tel: 0171–601 4878
Fax: 0171–601 5460

Bootlegging Information line/Schengen Information System (SIS)
UK Freephone: 0800 901 901

British Copyright Council
29–33 Berners Street
London W1P 4AA
Tel: 0171–580 5544

British Railways Board
24 Eversholt Street
Euston
London NW1 1VS
Tel: 0171–928 5151

British Standards Institute
389 Chiswick High Road
London W4 4AL
Tel: 0171–629 9000

CEDEFOP
European Centre for the Development of Vocational Training
Bundesallee 22
D-1000 Berlin
Germany
Tel: 49 30 884120

CEN/CENELEC (Joint European Standards Institutions; European Committee for Standardization; European Committee for Electrotechnical Standardization)
35 Rue de Stassart
1050 Brussels
Belgium
Tel: (322) 519 6871

Central Bureau for Educational Visits and Exchanges
10 Spring Gardens
London
SW1A 2BN
Tel: 0171–389 4697

Centre for Development of Industry (CDI)
52 Avenue Herrmann
Debroux
B-1160 Brussels
Belgium
Tel: (322) 679 1811

Chartered Institute of Patent Agents
Staple Inn Buildings
High Holborn
London WC1V 7PZ
Tel: 0171–405 9450

Chamber of Shipping
Carthusian Court
12 Carthusian Road
London EC1M 6EB
Tel: 0171–417 8400

Citizens First
UK Freephone: 0800 581 591

Civil Aviation Authority
CAA House
45–59 Kingsway
London WC2B 6TE
Tel: 0171–379 7311

Consumers in Europe Group
20 Grosvenor Gardens
London SW1W 0DH
Tel: 0171–881 3021
Fax: 0171–730 8540

Council of Europe, Point i
F-67075 Strasbourg, Cedex
Tel: (33) 88 41 20 33
Fax: (33) 88 41 27 45

Court of Auditors
12 Rue Alcide de Gasperi
L-1615 Luxembourg
Tel: (352) 43981

Department of the Environment
2 Marsham Street
London SW1P 3EB
Tel: 0171–276 3000

Department of Trade and Industry
(harmonizing standards)
Kingsgate House
Room 304
66–74 Victoria Street
London SW1E 6SW
Tel: 0171–215 5000

Department of Trade and Industry
Companies Division
10–18 Victoria Street
London SW1H 0NN
Tel: 0171–215 5000

Department of Trade and Industry
Competition Policy Division
Ashdown House
123 Victoria Street
London SW1E 6RB
Tel: 0171–215 5000

Department of Trade and Industry
(employment and training)
Ashdown House
123 Victoria Street
London SW1E 6RB
Tel: 0171–215 5000

Department of Transport
(marine and rail transport)
2 Marsham Street
London SW1P 3EB
Tel: 0171–276 3000

Department of Transport International Aviation Directorate
2 Marsham Street
London SW1P 3EB
Tel: 0171–276 3000

Developing Countries Trade Agency
St Nicholas House
St Nicholas Road
Sutton
Surrey SM1 1EL
Tel: 0181–643 3311

ECAS (Eurocitizen Action Service)
Rue Defacqz 1
1050 Brussels
Belgium

ECHO Information European Commission
3 Rue de Geneve
1040 Brussels
Belgium
Tel: (322) 295 4400
Fax: (322) 295 4572

Economic and Social Committee Secretariat
Rue Ravenstein 2
B-1000 Brussels
Belgium
Tel: (322) 546 9011
Fax (322) 546 9757

ERASMUS Bureau
70 Rue Montoyer
B-1040 Brussels
Belgium
Tel: (322) 233 0111

Eurochambres Conference of European Chambers of Commerce
5 Rue Archimède
Box 4
B-1040 Brussels
Belgium
Tel: (322) 231 0715
Fax: (322) 282 0850

EUROCITIES
18 Square Meeus
1050 Brussels
Belgium
Tel: (322) 552 08 88

Eurocontrol
Rue de la Fusée 96
B-1130 Brussels
Belgium
Tel: (322) 729 9011

European Association of Securities Dealers (EASDAQ)
PO Box 2
B1930 Zaventem
Belgium
Tel: (322) 27 20 78 70
Fax: (322) 27 20 83 06

European Bank for Reconstruction and Development (EBRD)
One Exchange Square
London EC2A 2EH
Tel: 0171–338 6000
Fax: 0171–338 6100

European Broadcasting Union (EBU)
Ancienne Route 17A
PO Box 67 CH1218
Grand Saconne
Geneva Switzerland
Tel: 41 22 717 2111

European Business and Information Centre Network (EBN)
Avenue de Terveuren 188A
B-1150 Brussels
Belgium
Tel: (322) 772 8900

The European Commission
Rue de la Loi 200
B-1049 Brussels
Belgium
Tel: (322) 299 1111

European Commission (London Office)
(*enterprise and international agreements general policy and information*)
8 Storey's Gate
London
SW1P 3AT
Tel: 0171–973 1992

European Council of Ministers Secretariat
Justus Lipsius
Rue de la Loi 175
B-1048 Brussels
Belgium
Tel: (322) 285 6111

European Court of Justice
Boulevard Konrad Adenauer
L-2925 Luxembourg
Tel: (352) 43031

EUROPE DIRECT
Freephone 0800 581 591
Internet: http://europa.eu.int/citizens

European Disability Forum
4 Rue de la Presse
0140 Brussels
Belgium
Tel: (322) 227 1121
Fax: (322) 227 1116

European Environmental Consultants
Rue Arthur Maes straat 82
1130 Brussels
Belgium
Tel: (322) 705 3260

European Free Trade Association
Rue de Varembé 9–11
CH-1211 Geneva 20
Switzerland
Tel: (22) 749 1111

European Foundation for the Improvement of Living and Working Conditions
Loughlinstown
County Dublin
Republic of Ireland
Tel: (3531) 204 3100
Fax: (3531) 282 6456

European Institute for Training in Fisheries and Agriculture (IEFPA)
Rue de la Science 23/25
B1040 Brussels
Belgium
Tel: (322) 230 4848

European Investment Bank
100 Boulevard Konrad Adenauer
L-2950 Luxembourg
Tel: (352) 43791

European Investment Bank
68 Pall Mall
London SW1Y 5ES
Tel: 0171–839 3351

European Monetary Institute
Postfach 10 20 31
D-60020 Frankfurt am Main
Germany

European Movement
158 Buckingham Palace Road
London SW10 9JR
Tel: 0171–824 8388

European Organization for Safety of Air Navigation – Eurocontrol
Rue de la Loi 72
B-1040 Brussels
Belgium

European Parliament
Information Office
2 Queen Anne's Gate
London SW1H 9AA
Tel: 0171–222 0411

European Parliament, Secretariat General
Centre Européen
Plateau du Kirchberg
L2929 Luxembourg
Tel: (352) 430 01
Also at Rue Belliard 97–43
B1047 Brussels

European Patent Office (EPO)
Erhardstrasse 27
D8000 Munich 2
Germany
Tel: 4989 23990

European Road Safety Federation
179 Avenue Louise
1050 Brussels
Belgium
Tel: (322) 646 6230

European Trade Union Confederation (ETUC)
Rue Montagne aux Herbes
Potagères 37
1000 Brussels
Belgium

EUROSTAT Publications
The Statistical Office of the European Communities
Bâtiment Jean Monnet
Rue Alcide de Gaspari
L-2920 Luxembourg
Tel: (352) 43011

Force Technical Assistance Office
34 Rue du Nord
1000 Brussels
Belgium
Tel: (322) 209 1311

FREE EU INFORMATION SERVICE
See Europe Direct

GLOBE
Globe International
50 Rue du Taciterne
1040 Brussels
Belgium
Tel: (322) 230 6589

Health and Safety Commission
Rose Court
2 Southwark Bridge
London SE1 9HS
Tel: 0171–717 6000

Institute of Trade Mark Agents
4th floor
Canterbury House
2–6 Sydenham Road
Croydon
Surrey CR0 9XE
Tel: 0181–686 2052

Interact News
Ambiorix Square 32
PO Box 47
B-1040 Brussels
Belgium

International Court of Justice
Peace Palace
2517 KJ
The Hague
The Netherlands
Tel: 070 302 2323

**International Credit Assurance
Association**
PO Box 16
7018 Flims-Waldhaus
Switzerland
Tel: 00 41 81 39 36 39
Fax: 00 41 81 39 36 28

International Road Freight Office
Westgate House
Westgate Road
Newcastle-upon-Tyne
NE1 1TW
Tel: 0191–201 4000

IRIS Traffic Control Crew
21 Rue de la Tourelle
B-1040 Brussels
Belgium
Tel: (322) 230 5158

Lingua Bureau
10 Rue de Commerce
B-1040 Brussels
Belgium
Tel: (322) 511 4218

**London Chamber of Commerce and
Industry**
33 Queen Street
London EC4R 1AP
Tel: 0171–248 4444

**Ministry of Agriculture, Fisheries and
Food**
Whitehall Place
London SW1A 2MH
Tel: 0171–270 8080

Official Publications Office (OOPEC)
2 Rue Mercier
L-2985 Luxembourg
Tel: (352) 29291

**Organization for Economic Co-operation
and Development (OECD)**
2 Rue André Pascal
75775 Paris
Cedex 16 France
Tel: 4524 82 00

Patent Office
Concept House
Cardiff Road
Newport
Gwent NP9 1RH
Tel: 01633 81400

PETRA, INFAPLAN
2 and 3 Place de Luxembourg
B-1040 Brussels
Belgium
Tel: (322) 511 1510

Road Haulage Association
Roadway House
35 Monument Hill
Weybridge
Surrey KT13 8RN
Tel: 01932 841515

Royal Commission on Environmental Pollution
Church House
Great Smith Street
London SW1P 3BZ
Tel: 0171–276 2080

Technical Centre for Agricultural and Rural Co-operation
De Rietkampen Galvinstraat 19
Ede
The Netherlands

Tenders Electronic Daily
Echo Customer Service
117 Rue d'Esche
L-1471 Luxembourg

The Treasury *(economic and monetary union and taxation)*
Parliament Street
London SW1Q 3AQ
Tel: 0171–270 3000

Union of Industrial and Employers' Confederates of Europe (UNICE)
40 Rue Joseph II
1040 Brussels
Belgium
Tel: (322) 237 6511

World Intellectual Property Organization
PO Box 18
34 Chemin des Colombettes
1211 Geneva 20
Switzerland
Tel: 4122 730 9428

World Trade Organisation
154 Rue de Lausanne
CH-1211 Geneva 21
Tel: Geneva 739 5019
Fax: Geneva 739 5458

Youth for Europe
The European Community Youth Exchange Bureau
2/3 Place du Luxembourg
B-1040 Brussels
Belgium
Tel: (2) 511 1510

Appendix V

Catalogue of Useful Publications

OFFICIAL EC INFORMATION

The European Commission Representation in the UK produces a catalogue of the publications that are available from its UK office. This is updated frequently. The material set out below was listed in its May 1998 catalogue, and is reproduced here to give an idea of the scope of information available from them and, incidentally, of the sheer volume of the work of the European Commission.

It should be noted that useful information is also available from the UK Government Departments, which also produce lists of publications.

BRIEF DESCRIPTION OF THE MAIN SERIES OF PUBLICATIONS

(FS)   *Factsheets*
are UK-produced booklets providing factual descriptions of Community policies and programmes and include names and addresses of UK programme managers/coordinators as well as relevant Official Journal references, where appropriate.

(BP)   *Briefing Papers*
are UK-produced booklets aimed at providing background information to academics and other informed audiences.

(RB)   *Regional brochures*
consist of a factual and illustrative description of the impact of European Community policies and programmes in the regions of the United Kingdom, including concrete examples of projects funded in each region.

(BR)   *Background reports*
are UK-produced surveys of particular Community policies, written in popular style as and when developments in European Community decisions are taken, with reference to source documents. Only selected titles appear on this order form. If you wish to receive them on a regular basis, please contact the Info Point of the European Commission London Office for a mailing list application form.

(OTM) *Europe on the Move* series
are Brussels-produced booklets providing general information on Community policies and programmes which include tables, statistical data and illustrations.

(ED)   *European Documentation*
Brussels-produced brochures, providing a more comprehensive overview (40 to 70 pages) on general aspects of the functioning of the European Community.

(CF)   *Citizens First*
are Brussels-produced booklets giving useful information on the rights of indivuals in Europe.

WHAT'S NEW?

Now available

THE EUROPEAN UNION – A GUIDE FOR STUDENTS AND TEACHERS – WHAT'S IT ALL ABOUT? WHERE TO FIND OUT MORE

The 2nd edition of the 40-page booklet sets out to help students and teachers discover the facts about the EU, its history and how it works. It also provides sources of further information – code number U1017.

1) THE EUROPEAN UNION: HOW IT WORKS, ITS HISTORY, INSTITUTIONS AND TREATIES

1a) General awareness and educational material

M1009	*Map*	The European Union – Member States, Regions and Administrative Units. Includes basic statistical comparisons between the individual EU member states, the USA and Japan (1996).
M1007	*Map*	The European Union – Member States, Regions and Administrative Units (1995).
Posters	*Posters – please see section 1b; 3 and 5*	Poster of the Commissioners; small map of the EU with travelling details; the euro sign and coins.
U1011	*What Exactly is Europe? – A classroom guide to the European Union*	This classroom guide intended for 11–14 year olds has illustrations, maps, poster and exercises and gives an overview of EU history, policies and programmes (32pp + inserts, A4, 1997; ISBN 1 86158 015 0).
U1010	*Europe Today*	A general booklet aimed at young people (16+) and the general public. It gives information about the EU, its history and current developments, decision making procedures, and the benefits for individuals (32pp, A4, 1997; ISBN 1 86158 016 9).
U6095	*Your Passport to Europe*	General information booklet aimed at 6–11 year olds including maps, word searches and quizzes (16pp, A6, 1995).
B6010	*Let's Draw Europe Together*	This workbook is intended for younger children and gives information in the form of puzzles and crosswords (52pp, A4, 1997; ISBN 92 827 8973 X).
B6128	*Exploring Europe*	This booklet is meant for young people. It briefly outlines what the EU has achieved, giving factual information about each of the 15 countries (84pp, A4, 1996; ISBN 92 827 7595 X).
U1017	*The European Union – a guide for students and teachers. What's it all about? Where to find out more NB: this replaces U6118, as below*	This booklet sets out to help students and teachers discover the facts about the EU, its history and how it works as well as providing sources of information about the EU (40 pages, A5, 1998, ISBN 92 828 2298 2).
U6118	*What's it all About – Where to Find Out More?*	(32pp, A5, 1995) – is no longer available – please see above for updated version.
U1012	*Europe at a Glance – How the UK Benefits From Being in the European Union*	Provides facts and figures about what the EU does for the UK in terms of funds and also rights and opportunities for its citizens (6pp, A4, 1997, ISBN 1 86158 020 7).

B6138   *The European Union:* (OTM) A question and answer style guide to issues such as
            What's in it For Me? citizenship and democracy as well as the "human" benefits
                                     of the EU: freedom to live in the EU, etc (36pp, C5,
                                     1996; ISBN 92 827 8108 9).

B6024   *A Citizen's Europe* (OTM) Provides a general description of the opportunities
                                     created by European policies for the citizens of the Union
                                     (56pp, C5, 1994; ISBN 92 826 6640 9).

B6142   *The European Union:* (OTM) A series of charts giving basic EU statistics such as
            Key Figures population, economy, standard of living, external trade and
                                     public opinion (44pp, C5, 1996;
                                     ISBN 92 827 7941 6).

B6140   *How Does the European* (OTM) A question and answer style booklet giving
            Union Work? information on the origins and aims of the EU, its budget
                                     and the principle of subsidiarity (28pp, C5, 1996;
                                     ISBN 92 827 8117 8

1b) History, Institutions and Treaties

B6143   *Seven Key Days in the* (OTM) Gives information about seven key dates in the
            Making of Europe history of the European Union (8pp, C5, 1997;
                                     ISBN 92 827 9853 4).

B6028   *Europe in 10 points* Sets out in 10 points to explain the nature and growth of the
                                     European Union (52pp, A5, 1995; ISBN 92 827 4844 8).

B6089   *European Integration* (ED). Describes the successes and failures of the European
                                     Community as it has evolved over the years (88pp, C5,
                                     1995; ISBN 92 826 9744 4).

B2000   *Europe From A to Z: Guide to* (ED) Provides quick and comprehensive answers about the
            European Integration main facts and policy areas surrounding the EU, arranged
                                     alphabetically (272pp, C5, 1997; ISBN 92 827 9419 9).

CD001   *Europe From A to Z: Guide to* As above, but in CD-Rom format.
            European Integration

B6121   *Serving the European Union –* Provides a description of the roles played by institutions of
            A citizen's guide to the the EU and how they work together (36pp, A5, 1996;
            Institutions of the European ISBN 92 77 93105 1).
            Union

ECMEM   *The Commission 1995–2000* Poster of the Commissioners including photos and portfolios
                                     (A4, 1996).

B6094   *The Commission's Programme* Presents the European Commission's work programme,
            for 1998 political priorities, new legislative proposals, the European
                                     Parliament's resolution on this programme and an address
                                     by the Commission President on the state of the Union
                                     (32pp, A5, 1998).

B9801   *The UK's Presidency of the EU* (BR) Provides general information about the priorities set
                                     out for the UK Presidency (6pp, A4, 1998).

B9706   *Brussels – Myths and realities* (BR) Provides details about the role of the European
                                     Commission and the other institutions (8pp, A4, 1997).

U5005   *The European Commission in* Provides an introduction to the work of the Representation
            Britain Today of the European Commission in the UK and the scope of its
                                     activities throughout the nation (16pp, A5, 1995).

U5035   *The Treaty on European* (FS) Factsheet. Explains the revisions to the Treaty on
            Union – The Meaning of European Union made by EU heads of government in June
            Amsterdam 1997, including pull-out pages on 10 points about the
                                     Treaty (32pp, A5, 1997; ISBN 1 86158 030 4).

B2003   *A New Treaty for Europe* Summarizes the revisions to the Treaty on European Union

	(second edition): Citizens' Guide	97 (16pp, 26.5 cm × 18 cm, 1997; ISBN 92 828 0812 2).
B8005	*Agenda 2000: for a stronger and wider Union*	Provides a summary of the Commission's proposals and strategy to meet the challenges of enlargement and reform of the Union's policies (4pp, A4, 1997).
B9702	*The Intergovernmental Conference (IGC) updated report*	(BR) Provides a progress report of the issues being debated at the InterGovernmental Conference (10pp, A4, 1997).
B6093	*I.G.C. 1996, Commission Opinion*	Commission Opinion – Reinforcing political union and preparing for enlargement (32pp, A4, 1996; ISBN 92 827 5857 5).
B6092	*Intergovernmental Conference 1996*	Contains the text of the Report on the operation of the Treaty on European Union, adopted by the Commission in May 1995 (106pp, A4, 1995; ISBN 92 827 4178 8).
BRP01	*The Member States of the European Union and the Intergovernmental Conference*	(BP) Provides a synopsis of the Member States' views on the possible institutional changes, discussed at the last IGC (72pp, A4, 1997; ISBN 1 86158 021 5).
B9801	*The UK's Presidency of the EU*	(BR) Provides general information about what the priorities are for the UK Presidency (6pp, A4, 1998).
B6021	*The ABC of Community Law*	(ED) Provides information on the Community's legal instruments, sources of Community law, the legislative process and system of legal protection (76pp, A5, 1994; ISBN 92 826 6293 4).
B6126	*Communication from the Commission – Services of General Interest in Europe*	Information on services of general interest in Europe (21pp, A4, 1996)

2) FUNDING / BUDGET

U5008	*Funding From the European Union*	This guide gives an overview of EU funding programmes, short case studies of funded projects in the UK, references to legislation and contact names in the UK and Brussels for further information. (48pp, A4, 1997; ISBN 1 86158 024 X).
B6132	*The Budget of the European Union: How is your money spent?*	(OTM) Describes how the EU budget is spent, how it is funded, how budgetary decisions are made and monitored, what action is taken to combat fraud (16pp, A5, 1996; ISBN 92 827 6658 6).
B6090	*The European Social Fund*	A booklet that describes the objectives and policy aims of the European Social Fund (16pp, A4, 1996; ISBN 92 827 3951 1).

3) THE SINGLE MARKET – FREE MOVEMENT OF GOODS, PEOPLE AND SERVICES

U5032	*Travelling, Studying, Working & Living within the EU* *NB: currently out of print*	(FS) This factsheet is aimed at providing practical information on travelling, studying, working and living within the EU (48pp, A5, 1997; ISBN 1 86158 018 5).
C2008	*Travelling in another country of the European Union*	(CF) This brochure provides information on the rights and responsibilities of individuals travelling within the EU (20pp, A5, 1997).
B6062	*Travelling in Europe*	(Folded pamphlet) Practical information when travelling in Europe, including bank holidays, duty free, VAT rates,

		speed limits as well as a map of the EU and administrative units (1997; ISBN 92 827 9954 9).
	NB: currently out of print	
C8001	*Living in Another Country of the European Union*	(CF) This guide covers EU citizens' rights of residence in other EU countries and their obligations (16pp, A5, 1996).
B6043	*The Single Market – 2nd edition*	(OTM) Describes the four freedoms of the Single Market and discusses single market policies, including trans-European networks and EMU (52pp, C5, 1996; ISBN 92 827 7822 3).
B3010	*Your social security rights when moving within the European Union*	A country-by-country practical guide about your rights and obligations in the field of social security, including sickness, maternity, unemployment and pension provisions in each Member State (222pp, A4, 1997, ISBN 92 827 5607 6).
B3007	*Consular protection for citizens of the European Union*	Provides details of entitlement to diplomatic and consular protection from the authorities of any Member State when travelling to non EU countries (8pp, 10×21 cm, 1997).
B9504	*The Schengen Agreements*	(BR) Describes the common policy on the crossing of external frontiers, including the conditions of entry of non-EU nationals and visa requirements, the fight against illegal immigration, and police co-operation (6pp, A4, 1995).
C2005	*Buying goods and services in the Single European Market*	(CF) Highlights the rights of EU consumers when purchasing goods and services in the EU (28pp, A5, 1997).

4) YOUNG PEOPLE, EMPLOYMENT, EDUCATION AND TRAINING

C8000	*Studying, Training and Doing Research in Another Country of the European Union*	(CF) This guide gives brief information on the rights of individuals to study, train and conduct research in another EU country, and the EU funding programmes available in these fields (16pp, A5, 1996).
C8002	*Working in Another Country of the European Union*	(CF) A guide to looking for work in other countries of the EU, as well as information on the rights of employees, the self-employed and retired people (16pp, A5, 1996).
U5032	*Travelling, Studying, Working & Living within the EU* *NB: Currently out of print*	(FS) This factsheet is aimed at providing practical information on travelling, studying, working and living within the EU (48pp, A5, 1997; ISBN 1 86158 018 5).
B6050	*Education and Training – Tackling unemployment*	(OTN) Highlights the educational, cultural and social exchanges and partnership programmes supported by the EU (8pp, A5, 1996; ISBN 92 827 5715 3).
B6045	*Creating Jobs*	(OTM). Explains the different measures the European Union is taking towards supporting job creation (8pp, C5, 1995; ISBN 92 827 5401 4).

5) FINANCIAL SERVICES AND MONETARY UNION

B6131	*When will the Euro be in our Pockets?*	(OTM) This booklet provides concise answers to the most frequently questions asked on this subject (20pp, C5, 1996; ISBN 92 827 8132 1).

B3002	*Talking About the Euro*	A question and answer-style guide for the general public on the euro (16pp, C5, 1997; ISBN 92 827 9917 4).
B5040	*Economic and Monetary Union*	This booklet describes the path to EMU and the scenario for the changeover to the single currency (24pp, C5, 1996; ISBN 92 827 7294 2).
B2007	*EMU and the Euro: How Enterprises Could Approach the Changeover* *NB: currently out of print*	A guide for businesses on changing over to the euro (34pp, C5, 1997; ISBN 92 827 9864 X).
BRP02	*Economic and Monetary Union – the Euro*	Sets out the issues of joining the single currency, looking at possible implications in the UK (20pp, A4, 1997; ISBN 1 86158 017 7).
B2005	*Euro 1999: report on progress towards convergence: part 1*	Recommendation from the European Commission for a Council Recommendation as well as summary of the convergence report (56pp, A5, 1998; ISBN 92 828 2982 0).
B2006	*Euro 1999: report on progress towards convergence: part 2*	Provides an assessment for each Member State of their progress towards convergence necessary for the transition into stage 3 of Economic and Monetary Union. This includes an evaluation of the compatibility of national legislation and tables and graphs on many economic factors in each country such as inflation, government debts (262pp, A5, 1998); ISBN 92 828 3271 6).
B1004	*Poster*	The euro sign and the celebration of 9th May (A1, 1998).
B1005	*Poster*	The euro coins and the celebration of 9th May (A1, 1998).
BN802	*Inf Euro*	Bi-monthly newsletter. The March 98 edition includes interviews, highlights preparatory work in public administrations and website details (12pp, A4, 1998).

6) THE ENVIRONMENT AND AGRICULTURE

B5095	*The European Union and the Environment*	(OTM) Provides an overview of all the measures taken at the EU level to protect the environment (40pp, A5, 1997; ISBN 92 828 1899 3).
B6130	*How is the European Union Protecting our Environment?*	(OTM) Provides brief answers to questions asked on the Community's environmental policies (16pp, C5, 1996; ISBN 92 827 8156 9).
B6134	*How Does the EU Manage Agriculture and Fisheries?*	(OTM) Provides brief but concise answers to the most frequently asked questions. (20pp, C5, 1996; ISBN 92 827 8149 6).

7) SOCIAL POLICY AND PUBLIC HEALTH

U5033	*European Social Policy*	(FS) This factsheet is aimed at providing factual information on what social actions are taken at the European level and how they affect the living and working conditions of citizens. (40pp, A5, 1997; ISBN 1 86158 023 1).
C2004	*Equal Rights and Opportunities for Women and Men in the European Union*	(CF) This guide covers the equal rights afforded by EU legislation in relation to employment and social security (A5, 16pp, A5, 1997).
B6090	*The European Social Fund*	Details employment and human resources development across the European Union 1994–99 (16pp, A4, 1996; ISBN 92 827 3951 1).

B6133	*How is the European Union Meeting Social and Regional Needs?*	(OTM) This booklet provides brief but concise answers to the most frequently asked questions (24pp, C5, 1996; ISBN 92 827 8141 0).
B3005	*The European Union and the Fight Against Drugs*	Gives information on the EU's role against drug trafficking and addiction (8pp, C5, 1997; ISBN 92 828 1068 2).
B3006	*The European Union in action against drugs*	Highlights the initiatives the European Union has taken in the fight against drugs (36pp, A4, 1997; ISBN 92 828 0426 7).
3001	*Video Europe Against Cancer*	1hr 36mn video on the Europe Against Cancer Programme, a cartoon film for children on cancer prevention, and films for teenagers explaining what cancer is and its relationship with our lifestyles (1989).

8) REGIONAL POLICY

B1002	*Europe Invests in its Regions*	(Folded pamphlet) Explains EU support for regional development and includes a map of eligible areas as well as questions and answers on regional policy (1997; CX 4 96 269 EN D).
B6133	*How is the European Union Meeting Social and Regional Needs?*	(OTM) This booklet provides brief but concise answers to the most frequently asked questions (28pp, C5, 1996; ISBN 92 827 8125 9).
B6038	*The European Union's Cohesion Fund*	(OTM). Provides details on the background and purpose of the Cohesion Fund to support the less prosperous Member States (8pp, C5, 1994; ISBN 92 826 8976-X).
U7000	*The North West*	(RB) A Region of the European Union (28pp, A5, 1995).
U7001	*East Anglia*	(RB) A Region of the European Union (20pp, A5, 1995).
U7002	*The South West*	(RB) A Region of the European Union (22pp, A5, 1995).
U7003	*Yorkshire & Humberside*	(RB) A Region of the European Union (28pp, A5, 1995).
U7004	*The East Midlands*	(RB) A Region of the European Union (28pp, A5, 1995).
U7005	*The West Midlands*	(RB) A Region of the European Union (20pp, A5, 1995).
U7006	*Scotland*	(RB) A Region of the European Union (32pp, A5, 1995).
U7007	*The South East*	(RB) A Region of the European Union (84pp, A5, 1995).
U7008	*The North East*	(RB) A Region of the European Union (24pp, A5, 1995).
U7010	*Northern Ireland*	(RB) A Region of the European Union (36pp, A5, 1995).

9) SPORT, LEISURE AND CULTURE

U5034	*Supporting Culture, Sport and Tourism* NB: currently out of print	(FS). This factsheet provides information on the support from the EU to preserve and enhance Europe's cultural heritage and traditions as well as to build upon its sport and tourism potential (40pp, A5, 1997; ISBN 1 86158 023 1).
B6125	*The European Union and Sport* NB: currently out of print	(OTM) Provides background information on EU activity within the sporting world (8pp, C5, 1996).
B6124	*A Europe of Towns and Cities – a practical guide to town twinning*	Highlights aid from the EU for twinning schemes and provides a country-by-country description of regional and local administrative divisions, including applicant countries (264pp, A5, 1997).

10) CONSUMER POLICY

B6141 *How is the EU Running the Single Market? What are my Rights as a Consumer?* (OTM) A question and answer style booklet giving information on the single market and consumer rights (28pp, C5, 1996; ISBN 92 827 8125 9).

B6072 *Consumer Rights in the Single Market* (OTM). Background information on actions towards the protection of consumers' rights (8pp, C5, 1993).

B9714 *European food policy* (BR) Highlights the European Commission's proposals for increased food safety (6pp, A4, 1997).

11) TRANSPORT AND TRANS-EUROPEAN NETWORKS

B6065 *Transport in the 1990s* (OTM). Background information on EC transport policy, the need or integrated networks, new open-market conditions, quota restrictions and trans-European networks (8pp, C5, 1993).

B9606 *European Transport Policy* (BR). Describes the main objectives of the 1995–2000 Common Transport Policy Action Programme including the development of trans-European networks, the promotion of public transport, safety and environmental considerations, transport pricing and liberalisation (6pp, A4, 1996).

12) INDUSTRY, THE ECONOMY, COMPETITION, SCIENCE AND TECHNOLOGY

B6060 *Competition Policy in the European Community* (OTM) A brief description of the benefit of a European competition policy such as low prices for consumers and control of mergers and take-overs (8pp, C5, 1992).

B6048 *The Information Society* (OTM) This brochure examines the economic and social implications of the information society for Europe and explains the EU's response. It also gives details of 10 European pilot projects (20pp, C5, 1996; ISBN 92 827 6238 6).

B5096 *Competition in Telecommunications: Why and How?* (OTM) This question and answer booklet examines the reasons and methods for deregulation of telecommunications (24pp, C5, 1997; ISBN 92 828 1314 2).

B3008 *The EU's Market Access Strategy – serving Europe's exporters* Describes the Market Access Database set up by the European Commission which provides information to exporters via Internet including market, customs and legislative information to combat trade barriers (16pp, A4, 1997; ISBN 92 828 1456 4).

B9503 *State Aids* (BR) Provides an overview of the legal framework and the EC's current policy and criteria for the granting of state aid (8pp, A4, 1995).

B9510 *Developing the Legislative Framework for the Information Society* (BR) Reviews the EC's legislative framework in the fields of copyright law, protection of databases and of personal data (4pp, A4, 1995).

B9516 *Small Businesses in the European Union* (BR) Describes measures taken at the EU level to support the development of small and medium-sized businesses and to improve their business environment (10pp, A4, 1995).

13) WORLD TRADE/RELATIONS WITH NON-EU COUNTRIES

B6136 *How Does the EU Relate to the World?* (OTM) A question and answer style booklet giving information on external relations and trade policy and common foreign and security policy (24pp, C5, 1996; ISBN 92 827 8165 8).

B6119 *10 Questions on the European Union and World Trade* 10 of the most commonly asked questions and answers (folded pamphlet, 8pp, 1995).

B6061 *The European Union and its Partners in the Mediterranean* (OTM) A brief summary of past and present EC policy towards the non-EU Mediterranean countries (8pp, C5, 1997; ISBN 92 827 5923 7).

B6040 *The European Union and Asia* (OTM) Provides information on relations between the European Union and Asia (8pp, A5, 1995; ISBN 92 827 5463 4).

B9511 *The Europe Agreements with Poland, Hungary, Rumania, Bulgaria and the Czech and Slovak Republics* (BR) Information on the commercial and economic provisions towards a free trade area, political dialogue and prospective membership of the EU (6pp, A4, 1995).

B9603 *The PHARE and TACIS Programmes Technical Assistance for Central and Eastern European Countries and the Newly Independent States* (BR) Provides information on the development of the two programmes and the allocation of funds for identified priority sectors (eg infrastructure investment) since 1994 (8pp, A4, 1996).

B9703 *The Enlargement of the European Union* (BR) Provides an overview of the applicant countries and an interim report on the effects on Community policies (8pp, A4, 1997).

B9709 *The Lomé Convention – a future after the Millennium?* (BR) Sets out the issues being examined to establish the future of the Lomé Convention with the African, Caribbean and Pacific States (6pp, A4, 1997).

14) SOURCES OF INFORMATION

UEYUK *Europe in Your Area* This guide gives contacts for European information within the UK (16pp, A5, 1997).

UEYSC *Europe in Your Area – Scotland* This guide provides contacts for information on Europe in Scotland (16pp, A5, 1998).

UEYWA *Europe in Your Area – Wales* This guide provides contacts for information on Europe in Wales (16pp, A5, 1998).

UEYSW *Europe in Your Area – South West* This guide provides contacts for information on Europe in the South West (16pp, A5, 1998).

UEYNE *Europe in Your Area – North East* This guide provides contacts for information on Europe in the North East (16pp, A5, 1998).

UEYNW *Europe in Your Area – North West* This guide provides contacts for information on Europe in the North West (16pp, A5, 1998).

UEYEM *Europe in Your Area – East Midlands* This guide provides contacts for information on Europe in the East Midlands (16pp, A5, 1998).

U6120 *European Union Information Directory of UK Sources* Directory of organizations and individuals in the UK who provide information on Europe locally (360pp, A4, 1995).

B6135 *Reader's Guide to Free Information from the EU* This catalogue provides a summary of the publications giving general information to the public. (68pp, C5, 1996; ISBN 92 827 8088 0).

WHERE TO FIND OUT MORE – INFORMATION RELAYS ON YOUR DOORSTEP

Most publications mentioned in this catalogue belong to categories/series produced in the UK and in Brussels/Luxembourg. A brief description of the types of publications available is provided. They are free (unless otherwise specified) and are available to the maximum indicated, according to current stocks. There may, however, be a charge for carriage for bulk orders. Delivery should follow within two to three weeks of receipt of your order.

The publications can be consulted and/or ordered through the following information relays, in your area:

European Resource Centres for Schools and Colleges hold extensive stocks of directories, journals, books and brochures on the EU and have access to up-to-date databases. They respond to the needs of schools and Further Education colleges.

Public Information Relays (PIRs) – Public libraries in the UK have set up a network of PIRs to provide the general public with access to information about the established policies and programmes of the EU in their locality. Members of the PIR receive much of the information and materials published by EU institutions and other relevant bodies and to have stocks to give away.

European Documentation Centres (EDCs) help universities promote and develop studies in the field of European integration. They enjoy privileged access to EU databases. EDCs also allow access for information on the EU and on its policies to the public and to students.

European Reference Centres (ERCs) are based in academic institutions and public libraries. They have small collections of EU publications for reference only. All are open to members of the general public and students.

European Information Centres (EICs) provide information to businesses. They have access to EU databases, including Tenders Electronic Daily which carries details of invitations to tender for public contracts. They have information about national and local regulations of direct interest to companies and some also assist companies looking for business partners in the EU through the Business Cooperation Network.

Carrefours – Information Centres for Rural Areas (CARs) provide a range of European information to all sectors of rural communities. They are able to access specific information about a particular region and assist in the search of European partners for local government, NGOs and the private sector. They also help place students seeking work experience in another Member State.

INFORMATION RELAYS IN THE UK

Greater London

BARKING: 0181 517 8666	(PIR)
BARNET: 0181 359 2883	(PIR)
BATTERSEA: 0181 871 7467	(PIR)
BEXLEYHEATH: 0181 301 5151	(PIR)
BRENT: 0181 937 3500	(PIR)
BRIXTON: 0171 926 1067	(PIR)
BROMLEY: 0181 460 9955 x250	(PIR)
CAMDEN: 0171 413 6531	(PIR)
CITY: 0171 489 1992	(EIC)
CITY: 0171 638 8215	(PIR)
CROYDON: 0181 760 5400	(PIR)
EALING: 0181 231 2248	(ERC)
EALING: 0181 567 3656	(PIR)
ELEPHANT & CASTLE: 0171 708 0516	(PIR)
ENFIELD: 0181 443 1701	(PIR)
HACKNEY: 0171 739 0610	(PIR)
HAMMERSMITH: 0181 576 5053	(PIR)
HARINGEY: 0181 365 1155	(PIR)
HARROW: 0181 424 1055/6	(PIR)
HOLBORN: 0171 955 7273/7229	(EDC)
ILFORD: 0181 478 7145	(PIR)
ISLINGTON: 0171 609 3051 × 217	(PIR)
KENSINGTON: 0171 937 2542	(PIR)
KINGSTON: 0181 547 6425/6402	(PIR)
LEWISHAM: 0181 297 9430	(PIR)
MILE END: 0171 775 3321	(EDC)
MORDEN: 0181 545 4089	(PIR)
RICHMOND: 0181 940 5529	(PIR)
ROMFORD: 01708 772 393/94	(PIR)
STRATFORD: 0181 519 6346	(PIR)
SUTTON: 0181 770 4700	(PIR)
UXBRIDGE: 01895 250 603	(PIR)
WALTHAMSTOW: 0181 520 3017	(PIR)
WESTMINSTER: 0171 629 2151	(EIC)
WESTMINSTER: 0171 389 4697/4723	(RES)
WESTMINSTER: 0171 641 1039	(PIR)
WOOLWICH: 0181 316 6663	(PIR)

South East

ASHFORD: 01233 812 512	(EDC)
AYLESBURY: 01296 383 245	(PIR)
BRACKNELL: 01344 423 149	(PIR)
BRIGHTON: 01273 678 159	(EDC)

BRIGHTON: 01273 691 195/6 (PIR)
CAMBERLEY: 01276 683 626 (PIR)
CANTERBURY: 01227 764 000 × 3111 (EDC)
CHALFONT ST GILES: 01494 874441 × 2249 (ERC)
CHICHESTER: 01243 777 578 (RES)
CHICHESTER: 01243 777 352 (PIR)
GUILDFORD: 01483 300 800 × 3312 (EDC)
HASTINGS: 01424 716 481 (PIR)
LEWES: 01273 481 151 (RES)
MAIDENHEAD: 01658 625 657 (PIR)
MAIDSTONE: 01622 694 109 (EIC)
MAIDSTONE: 01622 696 503 (PIR)
MAIDSTONE: 01622 605 704 (RES)
MILTON KEYNES: 01908 835 024 (PIR)
NEWBURY: 01635 40972 (PIR)
NEWPORT (IOW): 01983 527 655 (PIR)
NEWPORT (IOW): 01983 522 900 (RES)
OXFORD: 01865 271 463 (EDC)
OXFORD: 01865 810 182 (PIR)
OXFORD: 01865 395 150 (RES)
READING: 0118 931 8782 (EDC)
READING: 0118 923 3234 (PIR)
SLOUGH: 01753 577 877 × 134 (EIC)
SLOUGH: 01753 535 166 (PIR)
SOUTHAMPTON: 01703 832 866 (EIC)
SOUTHAMPTON: 01703 593 451 (EDC)
SOUTHAMPTON: 01703 832 958 (PIR)
WOKINGHAM: 0118 974 6261 (PIR)

South west

BATH: 01225 826 826 × 5594 (EDC)
BRISTOL: 0117 973 7373 (EIC)
BRISTOL: 0117 928 7944 (EDC)
BRISTOL: 0117 929 9148 (PIR)
CIRENCESTER: 01285 653 477 (CAR)
DORCHESTER: 01305 224 448 (PIR)
EXETER: 01392 214 085 (EIC)
EXETER: 01392 262 072 (EDC)
EXETER: 01392 384 281 (PIR)
EXMOUTH: 01395 255 352 (ERC)
GLOUCESTER: 01452 425 027 (PIR)
GLOUCESTER: 01452 427 204/270 (RES)
PLYMOUTH: 01752 305 906 (PIR)
POOLE: 01202 671 496 (PIR)
PORTSMOUTH: 01705 843 239 (EDC)
SWINDON 01793 463 240 (PIR)
TAUNTON: 01823 336 354 (PIR)

TRURO: 01872 272 702	(PIR)
TROWBRIDGE: 01225 713 727	(PIR)
YATE: 01454 865 818	(PIR)

Eastern

BEDFORD: 01234 350 931	(PIR)
CAMBRIDGE: 01223 424 022	(RES)
CAMBRIDGE: 01223 333 138	(EDC)
CAMBRIDGE: 01223 712 017	(PIR)
CHELMSFORD: 01245 495 921	(ERC)
CHELMSFORD: 01245 492 758	(PIR)
COLCHESTER: 01206 873 181	(EDC)
HATFIELD: 01707 284 678	(ERC)
HATFIELD: 01707 281 527	(PIR)
IPSWICH: 01473 232 041/2	(ERC)
IPSWICH: 01473 583 705	(PIR)
LUTON 01582 547 420	(PIR)
NORWICH: 0345 023 114/01603 625977	(EIC)
NORWICH: 01603 592 431	(EDC)
NORWICH: 01603 215 255	(PIR)
PETERBOROUGH: 01733 348 343	(PIR)

East Midlands

CHESTERFIELD: 01246 209 292	(PIR)
DERBY: 01332 255 398	(PIR)
LEICESTER: 0116 255 9944	(EIC)
LEICESTER: 0116 252 2044	(EDC)
LEICESTER: 0116 255 6699	(PIR)
LINCOLN: 01522 549 160	(PIR)
LOUGHBOROUGH: 01509 222 351/343	(EDC)
NORTHAMPTON: 01604 715 000	(ERC)
NORTHAMPTON: 01604 26774/1	(PIR)
NOTTINGHAM: 0115 962 4624	(EIC)
NOTTINGHAM: 0115 951 4579	(EDC)
NOTTINGHAM: 0115 977 4201	(PIR)
OAKHAM: 01572 723 654	(PIR)
QUORN: 01509 416 950	(RES)

West Midlands

BIRMINGHAM: 0121 455 0268	(EIC)
BIRMINGHAM: 0121 331 5298/414 6570	(EDC)
BIRMINGHAM: 0121 235 4545/6	(PIR)
BIRMINGHAM: 0121 446 3400	(RES)
COVENTRY: 01203 838 295 / 522 426	(EDC)

COVENTRY: 01203 832 325 (PIR)
DUDLEY: 01384 815 554/560 (PIR)
KEELE: 01782 583 238 (EDC)
KIDDERMINSTER: 01562 512 900 (PIR)
NUNEATON: 01203 384 027 (PIR)
SHREWSBURY: 01743 255 387 (PIR)
SOLIHULL: 0121 704 6974 (PIR)
STAFFORD: 01785 278 351 (PIR)
STOKE-ON-TRENT: 01782 202 222 (EIC)
STOKE-ON-TRENT: 01782 238 431 (PIR)
TELFORD: 01952 208 213 (EIC)
WALSALL: 01922 653 110 (PIR)
WARWICK: 01926 412 863 (PIR)
WEST BROMWICH: 0121 569 4911 (PIR)
WOLVERHAMPTON: 01902 322 300 (EDC)
WOLVERHAMPTON: 01902 312 026 (PIR)

Yorkshire & The Humber

BARNSLEY: 01226 773 935 (PIR)
BEVERLEY: 01482 885 081 (PIR)
BRADFORD: 01274 754 262 (EIC)
BRADFORD: 01274 383 402 (EDC)
BRADFORD: 01274 753 657 (PIR)
DONCASTER: 01302 734 320 (PIR)
GRIMSBY: 01472 323 600 (PIR)
HALIFAX: 01422 392 628 (PIR)
HUDDERSFIELD: 01484 221 975 (PIR)
HULL: 01482 465 940 (EIC)
HULL: 01482 465 941 (EDC)
HULL: 01482 466 843 (RES)
HULL: 01482 883 021 (PIR)
LEEDS: 0113 283 3126 (EIC)
LEEDS: 0113 233 5040 and 0113 283 3126 (EDC)
LEEDS: 0113 247 826 516 (PIR)
LEEDS: 0113 214 4072 (RES)
NORTHALLERTON: 01609 776 271 (PIR)
ROTHERHAM: 01709 823 614 (PIR)
SCARBOROUGH: 01723 364 285 (PIR)
SCUNTHORPE: 01724 860 161 (PIR)
SHEFFIELD: 0114 253 2126 (EICxEDC)
SHEFFIELD: 0114 222 7343/8 (ERC)
SHEFFIELD: 0114 273 4736 (PIR)

North West

ALTRINCHAM: 0161 912 5923 (PIR)
ASHTON-UNDER-LYNE: 0161 342 2031 (PIR)
BIRKENHEAD: 0151 652 6106 (PIR)

BOLTON: 01204 522 173   (PIR)
BURY: 0161 253 5054   (PIR)
ELLESMERE PORT: 0151 356 7606   (PIR)
GARSTANG: 01995 601 207   (CAR)
KNOWSLEY: 0151 443 3738   (PIR)
LANCASTER: 01524 65201   (EDC)
LIVERPOOL: 0151 298 1928   (EIC)
LIVERPOOL: 0151 225 5430   (PIR)
LIVERPOOL: 0151 225 8110   (RES)
MANCHESTER: 0161 237 4190   (EIC)
MANCHESTER: 0161 275 3770   (EDC)
MANCHESTER: 0161 234 1996   (PIR)
OLDHAM: 0161 911 4643   (PIR)
PRESTON: 01772 892 267   (ERC)
PRESTON: 01772 264 002   (PIR)
SALFORD: 0161 745 5846   (EDC)
SALFORD: 0161 736 9448   (PIR)
SOUTHPORT: 01704 560 090   (PIR)
ST HELENS: 01744 456 951   (PIR)
STOCKPORT: 0161 474 4524   (PIR)
WARRINGTON: 01925 442 889   (PIR)
WIGAN: 01942 827 627   (PIR)
WORKINGTON: 01900 603 744/605 311   (PIR)

North East

DARLINGTON: 01325 462 034   (PIR)
DURHAM: 0191 374 3041   (EDC)
DURHAM: 0191 383 4231   (PIR)
GATESHEAD: 0191 477 3478   (PIR)
HARTLEPOOL: 01429 272 905   (PIR)
JARROW: 0191 420 1711   (RES)
MIDDLESBROUGH: 01642 342 195   (ERC)
MIDDLESBROUGH: 01642 263 364   (PIR)
NEWCASTLE: 0191 261 0026   (EIC)
NEWCASTLE: 0191 227 4136   (EDC)
NEWCASTLE: 0191 261 0691   (PIR)
NORTH SHIELDS: 0191 200 5424   (PIR)
NORTHUMBERLAND: 01670 511 156   (PIR)
SOUTH SHIELDS: 0191 427 1818 x 2130   (PIR)
SUNDERLAND: 0191 514 1235   (PIR)

Northern Ireland

BALLYMENA: 01266 41531   (PIR)
BALLYNAHINCH: 01238 562 639   (PIR)
BELFAST: 01232 273 605   (EDC)
BELFAST: 01232 491 031   (EIC)

BELFAST: 01232 243 233   (PIR)
CLOGHER: 016625 49438   (CAR)
COLERAINE: 01265 324 029   (EDC)
OMAGH: 01662 244 821   (PIR)
PORTADOWN: 01762 335 247   (PIR)

Scotland

ABERDEEN: 01224 273 819   (EDC)
ABERDEEN: 01224 652 534   (PIR)
ALLOA: 01259 722 262   (PIR)
ARDROSSAN: 01294 469 137   (PIR)
AYR: 01292 288 820   (PIR)
BLACKBURN: 01506 775 335   (PIR)
CLYDEBANK: 0141 952 1416/8765   (PIR)
DUMBARTON: 01389 738 825   (PIR)
DUMFRIES: 01387 253 820   (PIR)
DUNDEE: 01382 434 336   (PIR)
DUNDEE: 01382 344 102   (EDC)
DUNOON: 01309 703 214/735   (PIR)
EAST KILBRIDE: 01355 220 046   (PIR)
EDINBURGH: 0131 650 2041   (EDC)
EDINBURGH: 0131 226 4531   (ERC)
EDINBURGH: 0131 225 5584   (PIR)
ELGIN: 01343 542 746   (PIR)
FALKIRK: 01324 506 800/2   (PIR)
FORFAR: 01307 461 460   (PIR)
GALSHIELS: 01896 752 512   (PIR)
GIFFNOCK: 0141 577 4976   (PIR)
GLASGOW: 0141 339 8855 × 6722   (EDC)
GLASGOW: 0141 221 0999   (EIC)
GLASGOW (G3): 0141 287 2850   (PIR)
GREENOCK: 01475 726 211   (PIR)
HADDINGTON: 01620 828 202   (PIR)
HAMILTON: 01698 453 402   (PIR)
INVERNESS: 01463 702 560   (EIC)
INVERNESS: 01463 235 713   (PIR)
INVERNESS: 01463 715 400   (CAR)
KILMARNOCK: 01563 526 401   (PIR)
KIRKCALDY: 01592 412 939   (PIR)
KIRKINTILLOCH: 0141 776 8090   (PIR)
KIRKWALL (ORKNEY): 01856 873 166   (PIR)
LERWICK (SHETLANDS): 01595 693868   (PIR)
LOANHEAD: 0131 440 2210   (PIR)
OLDMELDRUM: 01651 872 707   (PIR)
PAISLEY: 0141 889 2360   (PIR)
PERTH: 01738 477 060   (PIR)
SELKIRK: 01750 20842   (PIR)

STEPPS: 0141 304 1800   (PIR)
STIRLING: 01786 467 231   (ERC)
STIRLING: 01786 432 381   (PIR)
STORNOWAY (LEWIS): 01851 703 064   (PIR)

Wales

ABERYSTWYTH: 01970 622 401   (EDC)
BANGOR: 01248 383 874   (RES)
BARRY: 01446 735 722   (PIR)
BLACKWOOD: 01495 235 584   (PIR)
BRIDGEND: 01656 767 451   (PIR)
CAERNARFON: 01286 679 465   (PIR)
CARMARTHEN: 01267 233 3333   (CAR)
CARDIFF: 01222 229 525   (EIC)
CARDIFF: 01222 874 262   (EDC)
CARDIFF: 01222 382 116   (PIR)
CARDIFF: 01222 265 043   (RES)
CONWY: 01492 532 358   (PIR)
CWMBRAN: 01633 867 584 and 832 491   (PIR)
EBBW VALE: 01495 303 069   (PIR)
HAVERFORDWEST: 01437 775 248   (PIR)
LLANELLI: 01554 773 538   (PIR)
LLANGEFNI: 01248 724 701   (PIR)
LLANGEFNI: 01248 752 491   (CAR)
MERTHYR TYDFIL: 01685 723 057   (PIR)
MOLD: 01824 706 701 and 01352 754 791   (PIR)
MOLD: 01352 704 748   (EIC)
NEATH: 01639 764 230   (PIR)
NEWPORT: 01633 211 376   (PIR)
SWANSEA: 01792 205 678 × 4037   (ERC)
SWANSEA: 01792 655 521   (PIR)
WREXHAM: 01978 293 573/262   (ERC)
WREXHAM: 01978 293 573/262   (PIR)

OTHER INFORMATION

So many excellent books have now been published that I hesitate to recommend any. All the good publishers have EC/EU lists and have catalogues describing them: your choice will depend on your area of interest and possibly your budget. An extract from the Kogan Page catalogue is included here to show the scope of information available.

Much less formally published information and advice is produced by the large solicitors and accountancy firms covering these particular spheres of expertise. Trade and other associations can too provide useful publications. As always, it is vital to remember the importance of checking to ensure any information you read is up to date as the situation changes daily.

OTHER EU-RELATED TITLES PUBLISHED BY KOGAN PAGE

Access to Modern European Studies
JD Pratten and DWS Stevenson
£12.99
1 872807 61 5 208 pages

EMU Explained
Second edition
Reuters
£16.99
0 7494 2654 3 242 pages

EC Law
Arthur Lewis
£16.95
1 87280747 X 256 pages

Euromarketing
European Commission
£14.99
0 7494 2041 2 160 pages

Law of Industrial Subcontracting in the Euorpean Community – A Practical Guide
European Commission
£45.00
0 7494 2715 9 64 pages

Politics of the European Court of Justice
Richard Kruper
£9.99
0 7494 2607 1 64 pages

Secrecy, Democracy and the Third Pillar of the European Union
Tony Bunyan
£9.99
0 7494 2604 7 64 pages

The 1996–97 Inter-governmental Conference
Franklin de Housse
£9.99
0 7494 2611 X 64 pages

The EC/EU Fact Book: A complete question and answer guide
Fifth edition
Alex Roney (published in association with The London Chamber of Commerce and Industry Examinations Board)
£14.95
0 7494 2430 3 332 pages

The EU and Ethnic Minorities and Migrants at the Workplace
John Wrench
£9.99
0 7494 2605 5 64 pages

The European Social Charter: A Manager's Guide
Richard Pettinger
£11.99
0 7494 2715 9 160 pages

The European Union and Unemployment
Valerie Symes
£9.99
0 7494 2603 9 64 pages

The Single Market and Tomorrow's Europe
Presented by Mario Monti
Written by David Buchan, The Financial Times
£9.95
0 7494 2266 1 176 pages

THE SINGLE MARKET REVIEW

Series I: Impact on Manufacturing

Food Drink and Tobacco Processing Industry *DRI Europe Ltd / 0 7494 2305 6*	**£40**
Pharmaceutical Products *REMIT Consultants / 0 7494 2306 4*	**£40**
Textiles and Clothing *CEGOS SA / 0 7494 2307 2*	**£45**
Construction Site Equipment *W. S. Atkins / IFO / 0 7494 2308 0*	**£40**
Chemicals *KPMG / 0 7494 2309 9*	**£45**
Motor Vehicles *Ernst & Young / 0 7494 2310 2*	**£50**
Processed Foodstuffs *BER with Wye College / 0 7494 2311 0*	**£50**
Telecommunications Equipment *Analysys Ltd / 0 7494 2312 9*	**£40**

Series II: Impact on Services

Insurance *CEGOS / 0 7494 2313 7*	**£40**
Air Transport *Cranfield University / 0 7494 2314 5*	**£45**
Credit Institutions and Banking *Economic Research Unit / 0 7494 2315 3*	**£55**
Distribution *Coopers & Lybrand / 0 7494 2316 1*	**£45**
Road Freight Transport *NEA & CERT / 0 7494 2317 X*	**£40**
Telecommunications Liberalized Services *Bossard Consultants / 0 7494 2318 8*	**£40**
Advertising *Bocconi University / 0 7494 2318 8*	**£40**

Audio-visual Services and Production **£40**
KPMG / 0 7494 2320 X

Single Information Market **£40**
Analysys Ltd / 0 7494 2321 8

Single Energy Market **£45**
London Economics / 0 7494 2322 6

Transport Networks **£40**
AT Kearney / 0 7494 2323 4

Series III: Dismantling of Barriers

Technical Barriers to Trade **£45**
W.S. Atkins / 0 7494 2324 2

Public Procurement **£50**
Eurostrategy Consultants / 0 7494 2325 0

Customs and Fiscal Formalities at Frontiers **£45**
Price Waterhouse / 0 7494 2326 9

Industrial Property Rights **£40**
CJA Consultants / 0 7494 2327 7

Capital Market Liberalization **£40**
NIESR / 0 7494 2328 5

Currency Management Costs **£55**
IFO-Institut / 0 7494 2329 3

Series IV: Impact on Trade and Investment

Foreign Direct Investment **£50**
Economics Advisory Group Ltd / 0 7494 2330 7

Trade Patterns Inside the Single Market **£45**
CEPII & CIREM with FIES / 0 7494 2331 5

Trade Creation and Trade Diversion **£45**
CEPR / 0 7494 2332 3

External Access to European Markets **£45**
University of Sussex / 0 7494 2333 1

Series V: Impact on Competition and Scale Effects

Price Competition and Price Convergence   **£45**
DRI Consultants / 0 7494 2334 X

Intangible Investments   **£45**
RCS Conseil / 0 7494 2335 8

Competition Issues / 0 7494 2336 6   **£55**
London School of Economics

Economies of Scale / 0 7494 2337 4   **£45**
Economists Advisory Group Ltd

Series VI: Aggregate and Regional Impact

Regional Growth and Convergence   **£40**
DRI Consultants / 0 7494 2338 2

The Cases of Greece, Spain, Ireland & Portugal   **£50**
ESRI / 0 7494 2339 0

Trade, Labour and Capital Flows: The Less Developed
   Regions   **£55**
CERES / 0 7494 2340 4

Employment & Labour Costs in Manufacturing   **£50**
Cambridge Econometrics / 0 7494 2341 2

Aggregate Results of the Single Market Programme   **£40**
Technical University of Athens / 0 7494 2342 0

Results of the Business Survey

Eurostat / 0 7494 2344 7   **£45**

Available from book shops or directly from the publisher
Kogan Page Ltd, 120 Pentonville Road, London N1 9JN, UK
Tel: +44 (0) 171 278 0433 or Fax: +44 (0) 171 837 6348

Appendix VI

Information for Students and Academics

The European Commission UK Representation produced and circulated the list set out below of European Documentation Centres. They were established as a network to provide information particularly to help academics and students in higher education in and around London. There are similar sources of information and documentation elsewhere in the country (see Appendix V).

The European Commission has established a network of European Documentation Centres (EDCS) and depository libraries to assist students in higher education and academics. The following is a list of such centres in the London area. These collections contain official documentation, EC legislation, statistics and in some instances on-line databases.

EDCs for undergraduates

British Library of Political & Economic Science
10 Portugal Street
London WC2A 2HD
Tel: 0171 955 7273

Opening Hours
Mon-Fri: 0900–2120
Sat: 1000–1700
Appointment necessary

Queen Mary & Westfield College
Mile End Road
London E1 4NS
Tel: 0171 775 3321

Opening Hours
Mon-Fri: 0900–2100
Sat: 1000–1600

University of North London
The Learning Centre
236–250 Holloway Road
London N7 6PP
Tel: 0171 753 5142

Opening Hours
Mon-Fri: 0900–1900

Sat: 1100–1700
Appointment advisable

Information for researchers, academics and students can also be found on the Internet (see Apendix II).

Other centres

Westminster Reference Library
35 St. Martin's Street
London WC2
Tel: 0171 798 2036

Opening Hours
Mon-Fri: 1000–1900
Sat: 1000–1700

Dept. of Trade & Industry (DTI)
123 Victoria Street
London SW1E 6RB
Tel: 0171 215 5445

Opening Hours
Mon-Fri: 0930–1730
Appointment necessary

(Information on trade statistics & market intelligence)

Appendix VII

Community Legislative Measures

A DETAILED LIST OF COMMUNITY LEGISLATIVE MEASURES:

This list is reproduced from the Bulletin of the European Union Supplement 2/97 and it should be regarded as illustrative only, as further provisions have been passed since that supplement was produced. Other Bulletins cover different subjects. For example the Citizens Network Supplement 4/95 includes a valuable manual of Community Policy instruments of relevance to passenger transport.

EU legislation directly concerning commerce

There are a number of directives concerning the implementation of freedom of establishment and freedom to provide services:

(i)   wholesaling (Directive 64/223/EEC),

(ii)   retailing (Directive 68/363/EEC),

(iii)   commercial intermediaries, industry and crafts (Directive 64/224/EEC),

(iv)   commercial agents (Directive 86/653/EEC),

(v)   ambulant trade (Directive 75/369/EEC),

(vi)   teleshopping (Directive 89/552/EEC 'Television without frontiers').

Technical harmonization and the removal of barriers caused by differences in national product legislation (main regulations)

A first set of (horizontal) directives on product composition deals with *product ingredients*:

(i)   directive on authorized food additives (89/107/EEC),

(ii)   directives on colouring (62/2645/EEC and 94/36/EC),

(iii)   directive on sweeteners (94/36/EEC),

(iv)   directives on additives other than colouring or sweeteners (81/712/EEC and 95/2/EC),

(v)   directive on flavourings (88/388/EEC),

(vi)   directive on the inventory of the source materials and substances used in the preparation of flavourings (88/389/EEC),

(vii) directive on preservatives (64/54/EEC),

(viii) directive on specific purity criteria for preservatives (65/66/EEC),

(ix)   directive on emulsifiers, stabilizers, thickeners and gelling agents (74/329/EEC),

(x)   directive on specific purity criteria for emulsifiers, stabilizers, thickeners and gelling agents (78/663/EEC),

(xi)   directive on purity criteria for antioxidants (78/664/EEC),

(xii) directive on erucic acid (76/621/EEC).

The directives on *manufacturing methods* regulate various aspects of the production process:

(i)   directive on methods for the quantitative analysis of binary textile fibre mixtures (72/276/EEC),

(ii)   directives on methods for the quantitative analysis of ternary fibre mixtures (73/44/EEC).

A different set of directives contain *(vertical) product legislation for specific food products:*

(i)   directive on cocoa and chocolate (73/241/EEC),

(ii)   directive on sugar (73/437/EEC),

(iii) directive on honey (74/409/EEC),

(iv)   directive on fruit juices and similar products (93/77/EEC),

(v)   directive on fruit jams, jellies, marmalades and chestnut puree (79/693/EEC),

(vi)   directive on preserved milk (76/118/EEC),

(vii) directive on edible caseins and caseinates (85/503/EEC),

(viii) directive on natural mineral waters (80/777/EEC),

(ix)   directive on other water for human consumption (80/778/EEC),

(x)   directive on coffee and chicory extracts (85/59/EEC).

The internal market programme lays down the following *packaging* directives for the composition of materials and articles intending to come into contact with foodstuffs:

(i)   directive on vinyl chloride monomer (78/142/EEC),

(ii)   directive on testing migration of constituents of plastic materials and articles (82/711/EEC),

(iii) directive on ceramics (84/500/EEC),

(iv)   directive on plastics (82/711/EEC),

(v)   directive on regenerated cellulose film (93/10/EEC).

Several legislative measures relate to *product safety and hygiene*:

(i)   directive on hygiene and foodstuffs (93/43/EEC),

(ii)   regulation on contaminants in food (93/315/EEC),

(iii) directive on airborne noise emitted by household appliances (86/594/EEC),

(iv)   directive on toy safety (88/378/EEC).

The following directives and regulations with *labelling:*

(i)   directive on the identification of foodstuffs by lots (89/396/EEC),

(ii)   directive on nutrition labelling rules (90/496/EEC),

(iii)   regulation on spirit drinks (1576/89),

(iv)   directive on labelling of foodstuff prices (79/581/EEC),

(v)   directive on and resolution on the labelling of non-food product prices (88/314/EEC and Resolution of 7.6.88),

(vi)   directive on the indication by labelling of the energy consumption of household appliances (92/75/EEC),

(vii) directive on labelling and standard product information of the consumption of energy and other resources by household appliances (92/75/EEC),

(viii) directive on textile names (71/307/EEC),

(ix)   regulation on geographical indications and designation of origin (Reg. (EEC) No 2081/92).

The following legislation deals with testing, *certification and enforcement:*

(i)   directive on the verification procedure of purity criteria for certain additives (87/712/EEC),

(ii)   directive on the certification of the specific character of foodstuffs with a particular nutritional purpose (89/398/EEC),

(iii)   decision on the standing committee for foodstuffs (85/7/EEC),

(iv)   decision on the advisory committee for foodstuffs (80/1073/EEC),

(v)   directive on the official inspection of foodstuffs (93/99/EEC),

(vi)   directive on additional measures concerning the control of foodstuffs (89/397/EEC),

(vii) directives on methods of analysis necessary for checking the composition of cosmetic products (80/1335/EEC, 82/434/EEC, 83/514/EEC, 85/490/EEC, 93/73/EEC).

Elimination of border controls and abolition of border formalities

Several regulations and directives achieve the elimination of frontier controls:

(i)   regulation on Community Transit (3648/91)

(ii)   regulation on the use of TIR and ATA carnets in Community Transit (3237/96)

(iii)   regulation on the abolition of customs formalities at internal frontier crossings (3648/91)

(iv)   regulation on the elimination of transport checks at frontiers (4060/89)

(v)   regulation on the abolition of certain internal frontier controls into the field of road and inland waterway transport and their transfer to the Community's external frontier (4060/89)

(vi)   directives on exemption from VAT for the final importation of goods (83/181/EEC)

(vii) directive on the refund of VAT for taxable persons not established in the country (79/1072/EEC)

Indirect taxation (VAT and excises) — Main directives

(i)   Sixth Council directive on the uniform basis of assessment (77/388/EEC, last amended by 94/42/EC),

(ii)   Eighth Council directive relating to turnover taxes — refund of value-added tax to taxable persons not established in the territory of the country (79/1072/EEC),

(iii)   Thirteenth Council directive relating to turnover tax — refund of value-added tax to taxable persons not established in Community territory (86/560/EEC),

(iv)   directive on excise duties: general arrangements, holding and movement of excise duty products (92/12/EEC, amended by 92/108/EEC and 94/74/EC),

(v)   directive on the approximation of taxes on cigarettes (92/79/EEC),

(vi)   directive on the approximation of taxes on manufactured tobacco other than cigarettes (92/80/EEC),

(vii)   directive on the harmonization of structures of excise duty on mineral oils (92/81/EEC),

(viii) directive on the approximation of excise duty rates on mineral oils (92/82/EEC),

(ix)   directive on the harmonization of the structures of excise duties on alcohol and alcoholic beverages (92/83/EEC),

(x)   directive on the approximation of the rates of excise duty on alcohol and alcoholic beverages (92/84/EEC),

(xi)   directive on taxes other than turnover taxes which affect the consumption of manufactured tobacco (95/59/EC).

The liberalization of road transport

A quite extensive legislative framework underlies the creation of the internal market in road transport by trucks.

(i)   regulation on road carriage between Member States (881/92/EEC),

(ii)   regulation on inland cabotage for carriage of goods by road (3921/91),

(iii)   proposal for a directive on the admission of the occupation of road transport operator and mutual recognition of diplomas (74/562/EEC).

Relevant environment legislation

(i)   regulation on a Community eco-label award scheme (880/92/EEC),

(ii)   directive on packaging and packaging waste (94/62/EC),

(iii)   directive on batteries and accumulators containing certain dangerous substances (91/157/EEC).

Index